AUT

By the same author

A Man Under Authority (Kingsway)

Help Yourself to Health (New Wine)

AUTHORITY

The Imperative for Christian Leaders

Charles Sibthorpe

Highland Books

GODALMING
SURREY

First published in 1996 by Highland Books, Two
High Pines, Knoll Road, Godalming,
Surrey, GU7 2EP.

Cover Design by David Salmon

British Library Cataloguing-in-Publication Data. A
catalogue record for this book is available from the
British Library.

ISBN: 1 897913 26 5

Printed in Great Britain by Caledonian
International Book Manufacturing Limited,
Glasgow.

AUTHORITY

The Imperative for Christian Leaders

Charles Sibthorpe

Highland Books

GODALMING
SURREY

First published in 1996 by Highland Books, Two High Pines, Knoll Road, Godalming, Surrey, GU7 2EP.

Cover Design by David Salmon

British Library Cataloguing-in-Publication Data. A catalogue record for this book is available from the British Library.

ISBN: 1 897913 26 5

Printed in Great Britain by Caledonian International Book Manufacturing Limited, Glasgow.

CONTENTS

Acknowledgements

I want to express my thanks to those who have helped in the production of this book. Anne Vyce and Julian Perkins have worked on word processing and have soaked up all the pressures of meeting the deadlines required in book writing. Alison Kember has made sure that my English makes sense and my wife Joyce has thoroughly checked the text to confirm that all personal testimonies are accurate and honest.

I have greatly appreciated the creative input from my publisher Philip Ralli.

Foreword

What is Authority ?

Authority is the power and right to get the job done. In today's world there is a tragic shortage of authority in every area of society; it is also greatly lacking in the Church.

A pagan centurion caused surprise and amazement as he acknowledged that, when it came to matters of life and death, Jesus had greater authority than all the power of Rome.

The centurion's servant was sick and about to die, and he needed someone who had the power to rescue him from his desperate plight. The centurion knew his own limitations; strong though he was politically, spiritually he was void of power. In declaring, 'I myself am a man under authority,' he described his own area of command, but simultaneously recognised the superior power of Jesus.

The Bible shows clearly that Jesus demonstrated the almighty power of God throughout His life and ministry. However, in His final message to His disciples, He said these words, 'Anyone who has faith in me will do what I have been doing. He will do even greater things than these, because I am going to the Father.'

As it was spoken by Jesus, IT MUST BE POSSIBLE. He had demonstrated the power of God, but now He was delegating the same authority to us.

Then, why do we see so little power in the Church today? What are we lacking? How can we obtain this authority in our life and ministry?

SCRIPTURAL AUTHORITY

The Spirit of the Lord is on me,
because he has anointed me to
preach good news to the poor.
[Luke 4:18]

A WORD FROM THE HEART

The Church has its structures of
advancement and promotion, but
it cannot bestow divine authority.

Chapter 1

The Heart of the Matter

'It is God who calls. Man can appoint, it is only God who anoints. Here is a place where you can serve, only God can give you a ministry. You can watch me and learn from my experience, but it is only by continually meeting with God and seeking Him, that you will grow in faith and effectiveness. I can give you opportunity, but authority will only come when you bring your life under God's authority and also operate within a framework of human spiritual authority.'

The year was 1979, and it was during the month of June that I, together with my wife Joyce, set off for a week in Sussex. We had been invited to the Hyde, a beautiful country house, which had recently become the centre for the ministry led by Colin Urquhart. We had walked in the grounds, been overwhelmed by the spectacular colours of the rhododendrons and azaleas, had relaxed in a punt on the lake, and felt like royalty.

We had not however come for a holiday, but to hear from God with regard to our future. I had been born and spent all my life in Cornwall, never contemplating living elsewhere. We had been called to serve God in a full-time capacity two years previously, and were looking for the next step.

One evening after supper, Colin suggested that we join him in his study to chat and pray. After we had ranged around various topics, Colin suddenly turned to me and said, 'Charles, what is the deepest desire of your heart?'.

I drew in a breath to answer, but paused. I instantly knew the model answer, but I did not want to deceive myself, or Colin. I knew that my reply needed to reflect in truth what was genuinely in my heart. I gave my answer. Colin made no comment, but continued, 'If you could do anything you wanted for God, what would you do?' Again I paused. Was this the Spanish Inquisition? Once more I spoke out from my heart.

I have deliberately not given you my replies, because it would colour the response you need to make to the questions.

'I think it is time to pray,' Colin continued. We sat in silence for some time; we knew that this was not the time to bombard God with our hopes and desires, but to hear His voice. This was a new experience for Joyce and me. We had learned to expect prophecies in large meetings, but it had not occurred to us that God would speak at these more intimate times.

Colin spoke the words, 'My children, there are many people who have sought to bring revival to this nation and have not succeeded. I am seeking out a people who will bring my message of revival. They will not be the people that men would naturally choose. The distinguishing characteristic will be that they will be indelibly marked by the mark of my Cross.' The prophecy continued, but I regret to say I cannot recall anything more. I think I was stunned by the implications of what had just bombarded my ears.

As the prophecy ended we sat in awe-struck silence, until eventually Colin broke in and said, 'God has spoken. I know this word is not only for you, but a word to me and the ministry here. Perhaps God is telling you to leave Cornwall and join us here.' Colin then qualified his statement with the words that begin this chapter.

We heard from God, we returned to Cornwall, settled our affairs, packed our belongings into an enormous furniture van, bundled ourselves and our five children into the car and arrived at the Hyde.

It was there that I learned that effectiveness and authority in ministry does not stem from academic learning or technical training, but that it is primarily *a matter of the heart*. I do not deny the value of the formal, traditional method of training. In truth, however, development of spiritual authority cannot be received in the brain; it must take place in the heart.

The years that I spent working in the ministry with Colin Urquhart were some of the most creative in my entire Christian life. The heart principles that I learned changed my life, released me into ministry and are the abiding precepts by which I have continued to live my Christian life.

As I meet with leaders in the Church today, I find that the lack of understanding of these principles is the primary reason for weakness, fatigue and a lack of authority.

This book draws widely on the material used in my earlier book, *A Man under Authority*, which has been out of print for some time. With the present move of the Spirit which is sweeping the world, I have felt strongly that the heart principles that were expounded in that volume should again be available to all who seek authority and effectiveness.

Spiritual leadership and ministry is not a career choice, but a call from God; we do not operate out of a sense of duty, but out of the overflow of the heart; we are not carrying out pre-determined procedures, but responding to the prompting of God.

Authority will not come through diligent study, but through a fresh meeting with God. It will not be acquired by gaining experience in the work, but by allowing God to deal with the heart. It does not flow out of expertise, but on the river of divine love.

Three Questions

1.   What is the deepest desire of your heart ?

2.   If you could do anything you wanted for God, what would you do?

3.   Do you desire that your life be indelibly marked by the mark of the cross?

SCRIPTURAL AUTHORITY

Jesus said: 'whoever wants to become great among you must be your servant, and whoever wants to be first must be your slave
[Matthew 20:26-27]

A WORD FROM THE HEART

One of the key principles of leadership is the willingness to be a servant. The quality of every potential leader will be tested and trained through the simple, even menial, tasks which he is asked to do.

Chapter 2

Basic Principles

England has been called 'a nation of shopkeepers'. As one of the fourth generation of a family who ran three drapery stores, it never crossed my mind that I would work anywhere other than in the family business. I was also born into a very committed Christian family, where my involvement in God's work was as much taken for granted as my destiny in the family firm.

My parents, however, made it perfectly clear that my salvation was not hereditary, and I still remember, as if it were yesterday, kneeling with my father as a young boy to commit my life to Jesus, and receiving forgiveness and new life from God.

Nevertheless, I cannot remember a time when I was not involved at one level or another in Christian work and it would have been very easy to think that the call of God into leadership and ministry was inherited, just as the family employment was.

Called by God

This potential misconception was to change on a wet winter's evening, in a small Methodist chapel on St Agnes Beacon, Cornwall. Dr Denis Ball, who I had met first at Post Green in Dorset, had been invited to speak at a series of meetings in this isolated country chapel. When I arrived, with my wife Joyce and a car-load of friends, I was appalled at the poor attendance, and spent the first half of the service feeling angry that there were not more people present. However, when Denis began to speak I soon realized that God had appointed that evening specifically for me.

His message focused on Peter and the miraculous catch of fish. Peter's skill as a fisherman had failed, his own human weakness was exposed. He was now being called to take a step of faith and obedience. His friends were looking on. Would he commit his whole life and future into the hands of Jesus, or would he continue to live a more predictable lifestyle? The challenge was applied to the handful of us who had braved the elements and made up the congregation in that tiny Cornish village. For me this was more than a message in a teaching series being given by an anointed Bible teacher, this was the call of God. Would I be prepared to leave the safe and predictable and be ready to follow Jesus wherever he would lead? There could only be one answer for me.

God was calling me to commit my life in obedience and service in a way I had never done before. As Denis invited people to come forward for prayer, I leapt from my pew and was first at the front. I knew that it was important for me to act quickly, even though I would have found it more natural to have waited for others and followed them. But God was calling and I was eager to obey His call upon my life.

The next day I returned as normal to my work in the family business, but I knew inside that everything had changed. My destiny was not to remain within the predictability of buying and selling, administration and management; God had touched my life with His call and I was headed for a life of adventure with Him.

Several years were to pass before this became a reality.

The initiative always belongs to God. Jeremiah was called by God, despite his youth and his fears. 'See, today I appoint you over nations and kingdoms to uproot and tear down, to destroy and overthrow, to build and to plant' [Jeremiah 1:10]. God calls those whom He chooses. Therefore it is never a light responsibility to conclude that you have been chosen by God to live a life of service, ministry and leadership. This call will always be confirmed, if it's genuine. God will underline his command through the Scriptures and the confirmation of other mature Christians within the body of Christ.

A Servant Heart

Samuel had no aspirations of becoming a prophet when he arrived at the temple in Shiloh, he simply was there to serve in the temple. It says of him: 'The boy Samuel ministered before the Lord under Eli' [1 Sam 3:1]. God saw the trustworthy way in which he served and considered him to be the only one sufficiently reliable to receive and deliver a vital message to Eli. Greater responsibility was to follow.

One of the key principles of leadership and authority is the willingness to be a servant. The quality of every potential leader will be tested and trained through the simple, even menial, tasks which he is asked to do.

When the disciples were arguing as to who would have the prominence in His coming kingdom, Jesus said: 'whoever wants to become great among you must be your servant, and whoever wants to be first must be your slave.' [Matthew 20:26-27]

I found my own servant heart being tested in an unusual way. In January 1980 I travelled with Colin Urquhart to South Africa. My role was simply to be a travelling companion and prayer support; I was not involved in any preaching or teaching. I quickly discovered that no one really understood why I had come. As we travelled around, Colin was the important person and at times I was almost ignored. I well remember one place we visited where after two days, just as we were about to leave and were saying goodbye, our hosts had forgotten my name. Rather than glamour, here was humiliation. I went back to the Lord in prayer and was led to examine all the scriptures that speak about being a servant. Even to this day, I still mark all the verses in my Bible that speak of obedience and servanthood.

One reason that servant leadership is so important, is due to the fact that when mankind fell in the Garden of Eden, he was infected by a satanic desire to be equal with God. This is clearly seen in unregenerate mankind which is constantly trying to elevate itself above the Almighty. It infects us all and even among Christians is expressed in the desire for advancement and recognition. Paul E. Billheimer wrote:[1]

> This is why God uses for his greatest purposes only meek people, people that have been broken, emptied of themselves, delivered from their unholy ambition to remove God from the throne. This is why it has been said that whole, unbruised, unbroken men are of little use to God (Miller). Because the world worships suc-

1   Paul Billheimer, *The Mystery of His Providence*, Kingsway, 1983 p.67

cess, sometimes the only way God can break us is by failure. This may be a surprise to some, but God is more interested in the worker than the work.

Servanthood is not merely part of the promotion process, but is just as important for those who have already attained positions of responsibility and leadership. When I was in business, I made it a principle of my management not ask anyone to do anything I was not prepared to do myself. That did not mean that I had done it once — and was glad not to have to do it any more — but that I was ready to do it whenever necessary. I found this created a willing response in those who worked for me.

On the other hand, servanthood does not mean that leaders should become engulfed with tasks that others should be doing.

One who is followed

Jesus said: 'Come, follow me ... and I will make you fishers of men.' Then we are told: 'At once they left their nets and followed him.' [Mark 1:17-18]

When I was in business in Cornwall, we had three stores and employed about seventy people. As a manager, I was obeyed and felt that I had a loyal and hardworking staff. That was encouraging and flattering to my leadership and business skills. However, that loyalty was based more on monetary reward, than on voluntary action.

Leadership within the body of Christ is different. The people are not being paid, nor are they under any compulsion to submit. Clear direction on the one hand and compliance on the other, are vital, but the whole dynamic is based on the perceived spiritual authority of the leader not on 'carrot-and-stick' considerations.

A leader needs to give a strong lead and his life needs to be in harmony with the direction he is giving and the principles of God's word. The quality of his leadership, however, will ultimately be tested by the way in which people respond to it. This does not mean that he should try to please the people. Not at all! If he is a man-pleaser he will not be seeking primarily to please God, and will have consequently moved out from under God's authority and will not be worth following.

Judges 5:2 says: 'When the princes in Israel take the lead, when the people willingly offer themselves- praise the Lord!'

If no one is responding to you, then you have no spiritual authority and are not a leader. But if your life clearly bears the stamp of God, then there will be people who will offer themselves willingly.

Moving on with God

Paul was bold enough to say: 'Follow my example, as I follow the example of Christ' [1 Corinthians 11:1]. Leaders live under the challenge of continually moving on with God. This is not to say that every leader will be a spiritual giant; it is only necessary to be pressing ahead, which may mean that the leader is only half a pace in front of the people. Authority will depend upon a continuing walk with God. As He leads you on step by step, you will bring the people on in the same way, step by step. It is often a lonely path, because you are breaking new ground for others, but you yourself will only be following in the way that Jesus has already trodden.

Through discouragement and fatigue, leaders often find they have not remained out in front; consequently, their people have come to a standstill. You may hear someone say: 'My people have stopped moving on with God; they are stuck.' The truth of the matter is that he their leader is stuck.

As I travelled around the country with a team leading missions, I became aware of ministers and leaders who were working tirelessly and faithfully, and yet needed a fresh touch from God. It was this observation more than any other that drove the concept of the Hyde Leaders' Weeks. This was the ministry to leaders which

God led me to run for several years whilst working with Kingdom Faith Ministries in Sussex. The emphasis was on personal revival and the inner working of God in each person's life, so that ministry was released into new power and authority as each life was transformed by God.

The principles remain, and the need is still the same. Even though that specific ministry has ended and I now lead a local Church, the message remains as vital as ever for today's leaders, particularly in the light of the present move of God and the promise of revival.

Humble Heart

God described Moses as the most humble man who ever lived, and yet he was probably one of the greatest spiritual leaders of all time. How would you like to be leading those three million grumblers?

When a leader knows he is not capable of fulfilling his work in his own strength, it is a humbling experience. In fact Moses' response to the call of God at the burning bush was, 'Lord, please send someone else to do it.' This was not false humility, but a genuine reluctance born from the honest knowledge of his own human limitations.

The quality of this humility and reticence is found in many of Paul's writings, because he, too, knew he could only exercise his leadership under God's authority and with his power. Natural words and actions will not produce supernatural results in people's lives, and as the gospel is a supernatural work of God, it can only be activated through daily living faith. Paul's description of his mission to Corinth makes this very clear:

> When I came to you, brothers, I did not come with eloquence or superior wisdom as I proclaimed to you the testimony about God. For I resolved to know nothing while I was with you except Jesus Christ and him crucified. I came to you in weakness and fear, and with much trembling. My message and my preaching were not with wise and persuasive words, but with a demonstration of the Spirit's power, so that your faith might not rest on men's wisdom but on God's power.' [1 Corinthians 2:1-5]

An ambitious spirit is a great barrier to spiritual progress. Peter writes, 'Humble yourselves, therefore, under God's mighty hand, that he may lift you up in due time.' [1 Peter 5:6]

Right at the end of Paul's second letter to Corinth we find a pithy statement that recognizes the key to spiritual power: 'When I am weak, then I am strong.' [2 Corinthians 12:10]

Humility is a vital quality and reticence is not uncommon among leaders. However, reticence can lead to passivity, and a sense of inadequacy may also breed fear. We may well feel inadequate in our own human abilities, but that does not prevent us being strong in God.

Living under God's Authority

As I've said, the aim of this book is to explore heart principles that will release more of the presence, power and authority of God into your life and ministry. The account of the healing of the centurion's servant in Matthew 8 is pivotal when examining the essence of Christian leadership. In the ministry and leadership that we exercise, our authority stems from our relationship to the One under whose authority we act. The more of God's life, presence and authority there is in your life, the more of His power and authority will be released, through you, into the lives of others.

This was demonstrated perfectly in the life of Jesus and was recognized instantly by the centurion. Jesus lived constantly under the authority of His Father. He consistently testified that He only did the works that His Father showed him to do and spoke only the words given to Him from above. Jesus is our perfect example of the very best leader who has ever lived.

The basic principle that applies throughout is that leaders lead by example. The more deeply God works *in* you, the more powerfully He will be able to work *through* you. The more His Word is dwelling *in* you, the more His word of authority will come *out* from you.

Apply the Principles

1. *Called by God*
   When did God call you ? What has He
   called you to be ? Are you living in line
   with that calling ?

   1 Corinthians 1:26-29: 'Brothers, think of what
   you were when you were called. Not many of
   you were wise by human standards; not many
   were influential; not many were of noble birth.
   But God chose the foolish things to shame the
   wise; God chose the weak things of the world
   to shame the strong. He chose the lowly things
   of this world and the despised things- and the
   things that are not- to nullify the things that
   are.'

2. *A Servant Heart*
   Do you attach status to the tasks you
   perform, or are you willing to be a
   servant to your people ?
   Check your 'Servant rating' with your
   spouse, your children, and your fellow
   church leaders.

3a. *One who is followed*
    Willingly? ____ Reluctantly? ____
    Rebelliously? ____

3b.   *Moving on with God*
      Ahead of the people? _____
      About in step? ___
      Lagging behind?___

3c.   *A Humble Heart*
      Are you battling with pride ___
      or ambition? ___
      Does your humility tend towards
      reticence? ___
      Does this cause passivity? ____
      or lead into fear? ____

4d.   *Under Authority*   Are you ...
      Submitted to God? ____
      Submitted to His Word? ____
      Relying upon the Spirit?____
      Submitted to fellow-leaders?___

SCRIPTURAL AUTHORITY

Jesus said: 'For out of the overflow of his heart his mouth speaks' [Luke 6:45].

A WORD FROM THE HEART

What you are deep inside before a holy God who knows all about you, will be what you produce in your life and work

Chapter 3

A Heart after God

I was in my car driving up the M6 and listening to Andrae Crouch's *Live in London* concert album[2]. The volume was turned up and I was reliving the experience of having been at that concert myself.

The sound was washing over me and I was enjoying the vibrancy and energy of the music. A loud and rhythmic track had just finished and there was a spoken link before a softer, quieter song began. It was all about love for God. The lyrics were powerful.

The song was speaking to me in a way that it had never done before, in spite of the fact that I had listened to it many times. The line that really got through to me was this: 'You can take the one I love, I love the best…but I'm going to keep on loving you Lord.' Before I could take a grip on myself, I found that I was crying; although there

2   Andrae Crouch, *I just keep loving you, Lord*,
     Lexicon Music Inc 1978

was no one else in the car, I felt embarrassed. Questions were racing through my mind. Can I really identify with that statement? Do I mean, Lord, that if you were to take my wife Joyce in death, or one of the children, that I would continue to love you just as much?

I tussled with these questions as I drove on through the afternoon sunshine. Do I really mean it? I rewound the cassette, played it again, and pondered further. Deep within me I knew that the answer was: 'Yes, Lord,' even though that response had not been put to the test.

It is amazing how fundamental issues are often not confronted until someone asks a seemingly simple question. 'Do you truly love me more than these?' was the question the brought Peter's life back on track after he had denied Jesus. The episode just recounted caused me to ask serious questions concerning my love for God and His priority in my life. I believe that it is vital for you to address this issue and to have resolved it in your mind and heart, if you are to have a foundation of security and authority to minister out of.

God knew the things that would compete for the hearts of mankind. That is why He gave such a direct command to His covenant people when he said to them: 'Love the Lord your God with all your heart and with all your soul and with all your strength' [Deuteronomy 6:5].

The things that control your heart will dominate your thoughts, and your thoughts will govern your life. I found this quotation in a book some years ago, 'What you think about when you are free to think about anything you want, that is what you are or will soon become.' What you are deep inside, before a Holy God who knows all about you, will be what you produce in your life and work. It is not so much what you say that affects others, but what you are.

The one who has captured your heart motivates your whole life. Jesus said: 'For out of the overflow of his heart his mouth speaks.' [Luke 6:45]

David - a man after God's own heart

It seems strange that God should say to Samuel that He had, 'sought out a man after his own heart and appointed him leader of his people.'[1 Samuel 13:14] Surely God knew that David was going to commit adultery with Bathsheba and send her husband Uriah to his death.

It was not perfection that God was looking for, but someone who was sensitive to sin. If God has captured your heart, He knows that He will find a tender, responsive and repentant heart when He needs to correct, or confront you with, your sin,

See how David reacted, when Nathan faced him with his adultery and murder. His immediate response was, 'I have sinned against the Lord'

[2 Samuel 12:13]. His love was centred upon God. The pain of how his sin displeased God is evident in Psalm 51: 'Do not cast me from your presence' (v. 11); 'Save me from bloodguilt, O God' (v. 14); 'The sacrifices of God are a broken spirit; a broken and contrite heart, O God, you will not despise' (v. 17).

The contrast between Saul and David is striking—both of them sinned and failed, but whereas Saul was rejected and set aside by God, David came through to restoration and forgiveness. What made the difference?

Saul was full of self-justification when Samuel confronted him with his sin [1 Sam 15:13-35], and even his attempted repentance was tainted with self-protection as he said, 'I have sinned. But please honour me before the elders of my people' (v. 30).

Saul's love was centred upon himself and self-pleasing; 1 Chronicles 10:13 writes his epitaph thus: 'Saul died because he was unfaithful to the Lord; he did not keep the word of the Lord.' God found him unreliable in his heart and it was this that led to his final rejection and loss of kingship.

When the going gets tough, your actions will reveal where you have really placed your love and trust. Your love for God is vital.

A Heart after God -
will produce obedience to God's Word

One lady who worked with us at the Hyde was very free and demonstrative when praising and worshipping God. Joyce, who admired her greatly, was challenged by this freedom and spoke to Colin about it. 'I wish I loved the Lord as much as she does,' Joyce said. To which Colin replied, 'The test of her love is not shown by her freedom in worship, but her obedience to God's will.'

Jesus said: 'If anyone loves me, he will obey my teaching' [John 14:23]. It is important to check out the depth of your love for God by looking carefully at the extent of your obedience.

Love that goes deep will touch the emotions, but it will go beyond that to determine behaviour. It is not a sign of weakness to be so overwhelmed by love for God that tears are shed. Nor is it unseemly to be so in love with Jesus that you are 'lost in wonder, love and praise'. True love for God will be warm, and will be expressed in joy and abandonment during times of worship and praise, but also in a life that is marked by its obedience to the teachings of Jesus.

That does not mean following a legalistic code of religious rules, a practice of the Pharisees that was firmly condemned by Jesus. It does mean joyful obedience to all that Jesus taught.

How much of your behaviour is the expression of your love for God?

A Heart after God -
brings blessing to marriage and family

The greatest need for a wife is to have a husband with a heart after God. This means that he will love God more than his wife; however, she will not suffer, because such a man will give her greater love than if the order was reversed. (It may take you a moment or two to digest that last sentence.) It is just the same for the husband, who needs a wife who loves God more than she loves him. This may seem strange logic, but I assure you that it works.

It will also mean that disputes are solved by seeking the mind and will of God rather than through contention and argument.

Here is a tremendous promise for those with children: 'Blessed is the man who fears the Lord, who finds great delight in his commands. His children will be mighty in the land.'[Psalm 112:1-2] We are greatly privileged to have all our children following the Lord. The four who are married all have partners who are believers and those with children are bringing them up to love and serve the Lord.

When I think of the way that God has worked in our family, I am overwhelmed by His grace. It is a joy to be able to fellowship with your own children, to see them totally involved in serving God and 'on fire' for Him. Although time dulls the memory, it is not so long ago that Joyce and I were daily declaring the promises of God over our children as they battled with His claims on their lives— the principles that are being shared in this book work because God is faithful to *all* His promises.

A Heart after God -
will be our response to God's love for us

How do you arrive at the place where you know your love for God is the most powerful force in the whole of your life?

One of the reasons why love for God in so many is not as strong as they would want, is because they have not fully received the love God has for them. You need love from God in order to love Him. You need love from God in order to love others. Natural human love will be inadequate on both counts.

Many people have complete assurance that they have received new life and salvation in Christ, and yet have no deep understanding or confidence that they are really loved by God.

Insecurity is one of the most powerful of emotions and it can weaken and undermine your relationships, both with God and man. The healing of insecurities comes not so much from understanding the hurts and pains of childhood, as by a revelation that you are loved and accepted by God today.

John says: 'We love because he first loved us' [1 John 4:19], and 'How great is the love the Father has lavished on us, that we should be called children of God! And that is what we are!' [1 John 3:1].

I was taking a conference in the North of England and speaking on this theme. I was giving the illustration of how I enjoyed picking up my children when they were young and sitting them on my knee in a place of warmth, love and security. I then likened this to the way God shows his love to us. At the end of the meeting a lady came to me in great distress. She told me that she could never remember either of her parents ever picking her up and loving her as I had described. This had created a tremendous barrier to her receiving the love of God; what's more, she was a nun living in a convent where expressions of human love were limited. She desperately wanted to experience the healing love of God in her life. As I prayed, I reached out to God for a miracle and asked Him to come and reveal his love to her in all its fullness. There was nothing to be seen immediately except a release of tears. I had not realised that she had not been able to cry for many years. Later, I received a letter from this nun telling me of how God had come to her a few days later, placed His arms around her and brought love and healing deep within.

God has chosen you because He loves you; because He loves you, He has made you one of the family; and that means that you belong to Him and He belongs to you!

For many of those involved in ministry such insecurity can create tremendous pressure. Christians leaders are among some of the most insecure people I have met. Many are working day and night because they feel so unloved and uncertain of God's care for them. They feel that if they work hard enough and serve others selflessly enough, then they will earn His love and approval.

That is a tragedy, because there is no way you can earn anything from God. What you are, and what you will become, is entirely dependent upon His grace and love. You can merit none of His favour. Endeavouring to do so proves counter-productive to God's real purposes: your own restlessness and doubt gets disseminated, rather than the peace and love of God.

In God's plan, we all need to have been baptised in the Holy Spirit (and to know that we have been), 'because those who are led by the Spirit of God are sons of God. For you did not receive a spirit that makes you a slave again to fear, but you received the Spirit of sonship. And by him we cry 'Abba, Father'. The Spirit himself testifies with our spirit that we are God's children' [Romans 8:14-16].

Neglect the work of the Holy Spirit, and your walk with God will become cold and lifeless. The reality of our faith is that it is spiritual and supernatural. Therefore, the knowledge of salvation comes by the work of the Holy Spirit. The power to live your life as God's child comes through the infilling of the Holy Spirit. The revelation of God's love and fatherhood is also by the Holy Spirit.

Luther once said: 'The longest journey in the world is from a man's head to his heart.' I know that the revelation of God's love for me took that 15-inch journey when God filled me with his Holy Spirit.

A heart after God -
sets me free from human pressure

'There is no fear in love. But perfect love drives out fear.' [1 John 4:18]

'Fear of man will prove to be a snare.' [Proverbs 29:25]

'The fear of the Lord is the beginning of wisdom.' [Proverbs 9:10]

Love for God is so important: it can control other forces that seek to manipulate our lives. Your love for God and the revelation of His love for you need to be the most powerful forces in your life. Then you will not be prey to every pressure put upon you by people, because the power of the love of God will control your thoughts and actions. You will be set free to hear God, to obey Him and to lead others to know and love God.

A Heart after God -
will help me receive healing from God

Over the past few years I have had close contact with a number of people recovering from drug and alcohol dependency. Many of these have come for help with their problem because they have become Christians and want to break free from their old life. I have observed that those whose commitment to Christ has produced a deep love for Him and a heart after God have made much more rapid progress than those with a lesser commitment.

The opposite is also true: a friend of mine who ran a drug re-hab centre was asked by a minister to take in a man with severe alcohol problems. Having interviewed this man, my friend refused to enrol him on the programme. Why? Because he was not serious with God. The minister was surprised, and a little hurt, to have his man re-fused, but subsequent events proved my friend right.

When God's love is truly established and growing in our hearts, He is able to perform his work of transformation within us.

A heart after God -
will produce a passion for souls

When we are living in the security of the knowledge of God's love for us, and we know that He has the first place in our hearts, it will deliver us from self-centredness and we will be able to gain God's perspective on the world around us.

We are surrounded by a dying world who are 'without hope and without God in the world' [Ephesians 2:12], and who are going to a lost eternity and everlasting torment. This should motivate us to action. I believe that the mark of the final end-time revival will be a mighty ingathering of souls.

Many have been mightily touched by God recently; I have been reading a book by Andy and Jane Fitzgibbon from Sunderland in which they write: 'In our recent experience of spiritual refreshing, when people have fallen radically and totally in love with Christ, we have seen the most amazing fruitfulness'[3]. The desire to become fruitful follows naturally from a relationship of

3   A & J Fitz-Gibbon, *The Kiss of Intimacy*, Monarch 1995

closeness to Jesus. Those whose hearts have been renewed in the power of the Spirit of God long to see many others brought into the kingdom of God.

What is the depth of your love for God? Do you really know how great God's love is for you? Will the strength of your love for Him and the power of His love for you keep your life strong in the face of all opposition?

You need to know the answers to those questions. Jesus needed to know the depth of Peter's response. That is why he was so persistent in the encounter recorded in John 21:15-18.

'Simon son of John, do you truly love me more than these?' 'Yes Lord,' he said, 'you know that I love you.' Jesus said, 'Feed my lambs.' Again Jesus said, 'Simon son of John, do you truly love me?' He answered, 'Yes, Lord, you know that I love you.' Jesus said, 'Take care of my sheep.' The third time he said to him 'Simon son of John, do you love me?' Peter was hurt because Jesus asked him the third time, 'Do you love me?' He said, 'Lord, you know all things; you know that I love you.' Jesus said, 'Feed my sheep. I tell you the truth, when you were younger you dressed yourself and went where you wanted; but when you are old you will stretch out your hands, and someone else will dress you and lead you where you do not want to go.'

It was of the utmost importance that both Jesus and Peter knew the extent of their love for each other. As far as Jesus was concerned that was not in doubt, but Peter's love had been tested already and been found wanting. The questions were clear and penetrating, and the answers were honest. This was not only the prelude to mighty blessing for thousands on the day of Pentecost, but it also led to great personal cost for Peter and eventual martyrdom in the cause of Christ.

Today, God is still looking for men and women today who will give themselves wholeheartedly to love and serve Him and to be His anointed servants. It is a costly and demanding commitment, as was Peter's, and requires a love and perseverance so strong that it will stop at nothing for the sake of the Lord.

We desire to see powerful and dynamic demonstrations of God's power in our work and ministry, we seek to be people of faith. However Paul writes, 'The only thing that counts is faith expressing itself through love.'

Developing a Heart after God

1. It is important to give time each day to worship and to expressing in words as well as in song your love for God.

2. True love for God will strengthen your marriage and your family life. Take time to tell your spouse of your love and commitment, and also your children.

3. When God has the right place in your life and you are living only to please Him, it will take the pressure off you. Check things out, if you are finding yourself under stress at this time.

4. The person with a heart after God will have a love for those who are not yet believers. If you have grown cold towards the lost, ask God to re-kindle your love today.

SCRIPTURAL AUTHORITY

'The men turned away and went toward Sodom, but Abraham remained standing before the Lord' (Gen 18:22).

A WORD FROM THE HEART

Unless you acknowledge the fact that you are called by God to stand in his holy presence every day, ... you will fall victim to the pressures of life

Chapter 4

Standing Before God

I have often been amused by a story Colin Urquhart tells from his parish experience at Luton. Colin became so involved with the personal problems and needs of his congregation, that by the time Saturday night came he could think of nothing else. Everything within him wanted to stand up in the pulpit on Sunday and sort the people out! But was this what God wanted?

Colin found a way of dealing with the situation. He would go into the church, lock the door and climb into the pulpit. He would view the empty pews and, with a mental picture of all the people who would fill them the next day, he would speak out just what they needed to hear! Having got it all out of his system, Colin would then step down from the pulpit, sink to his knees at the altar rail and cry out: 'All right, Lord, now what do you want to say?'

I have found this to be a vital principle in my own ministry, now that I am a pastor. Five years ago I, together with my wife, planted Living Waters Church in Clevedon. I too stand before the people each Sunday and need to bring them a word from God, not just my reactions to the events of the past week.

Some years ago I met Chuck Smith, who was then the pastor of Calvary Chapel, Costa Mesa, California. He was speaking at a ministers' gathering and giving us the benefit of his vast experience. I remember him telling how he would rise very early on a Sunday morning and pray through the message for the morning service. He expressed it this way, 'I rise early to pray and prepare; in fact, I just pray right through until I am standing in front of my people.' At the time it seemed strange to me, but that is how I would now describe my Sunday mornings. I too rise early to stand before God on behalf of the people and to pray my way right into the pulpit!

We are called primarily to stand before the Lord and to minister to him. In the early books of the Bible, this principle is seen in the work of the levitical priests. 'At that time the Lord set apart the tribe of Levi to carry the ark of the covenant of the Lord, to stand before the Lord to minister and to pronounce blessings in his name, as they still do today' (Deut 10:8).

The sobering fact is this: unless ministry is pleasing to God it will be powerless. Have you been called to please God, to please the people or to please yourself? That question needs careful consideration.

Unless you acknowledge the fact that you are called by God to stand in His holy presence every day and to worship and serve Him, you will fall victim to all the pressures of life.

Standing before God -
brings security to the people

I do not believe that we ever reach a situation where we pray too much; therefore we all come under conviction when our prayer life is being placed under the microscope. Nevertheless, the importance you give to prayer will have a great impact on the effectiveness of your ministry. The security of the people depends largely upon the prayer life of their leader. I like the account of Moses' prayer habits:

> And whenever Moses went out to the tent, all the people rose and stood at the entrance to their tents watching Moses until he entered the tent. As Moses went into the tent, the pillar of cloud would come down and stay at the entrance, while the Lord spoke with Moses.
> [Exodus 33:8-9]

I believe that there is great strength in knowing that your leader is predominantly one who prays. I like the picture of the people in Moses' day standing at the entrance of their tents. The account in Exodus creates a wonderful atmosphere of peace and confidence reigning over the camp. Why? Because the man of God is praying.

I believe that prayer is the most important part of the life of my Church. I seek to encourage a personal prayer life in each individual, and would expect all the fully committed people to attend at least one Prayer meeting during the week. We meet at least five times each week for Prayer, once in the early morning, one evening, a day time Prayer Workshop and twice on Sundays, before each service.

Standing before God - keeps repentance fresh

As I stand before God each day and in worship and waiting in His presence, I am in the ideal place for Him to convict me of sin or of anything that is displeasing to Him. This is a very healthy place to be; it is not to be introspective, but rather to be open and willing to change.

When Isaiah went into the temple 'in the year that King Uzziah died', he must have been puzzled by the sad end of a king who had been greatly used by God. Why had Uzziah disobeyed God by burning incense in the temple, which was a privilege reserved solely for the priests? Why had God struck him down with leprosy? What a very severe punishment! Had Isaiah felt aggrieved with God, it would be easy to sympathize with him; but Isaiah did not argue or reason with God.

He went into the temple to worship Him and to stand in his presence.

He recalled, 'I saw the Lord seated on a throne, high and exalted' [Isaiah 6:1] and then went on to describe the majestic scene before him. When you are facing situations that you cannot understand and are looking for answers where there seem to be none, God holds the key. His holy presence did not give human answers but it transformed Isaiah's whole perspective.

As one involved in ministry you need constantly to withdraw from the hurly-burly and demands of your work to spend time alone with God. Isaiah was so overwhelmed by the greatness and glory of God that a dramatic transformation took place. The vision of a holy God caused him to acknowledge his unholiness and utter weakness. 'Woe to me,' he cried. 'I am ruined! for I am a man of unclean lips' [v.5].

Isaiah's repentance released God's forgiveness and cleansing. The seraph flew to the altar, removed the live coal and touched Isaiah's mouth saying, 'See, this has touched your lips; your guilt is taken away and your sin atoned for' [v.7].

Standing before God -
develops consistency and maturity

Too often, I meet ministers and leaders who are discouraged and battered by their circumstances. It does very little good to attempt to analyze the situation or to seek answers for their problems. It is far more important to point them directly to the living God. When a man has stood before God and had a fresh encounter with Him, he will often have already received the answer to his dilemma. To stand before God and hear His voice more clearly than the voice of man is to be reassured by His love and peace, whatever the situation. It will provide protection from the erosive effects of the surrounding sin and darkness.

The story of Samuel from the Old Testament is a powerful illustration. It begins with the fascinating account of Hannah praying for the gift of a baby boy, and then reveals how she gave the child back to God when her prayer had been answered.

The environment of Samuel's training for ministry [1 Samuel 2] was far from ideal. Eli was very old and had lost his grip on the job. His two sons Hophni and Phinehas were living lives of sin and disobedience to God. 'They had no regard for the Lord' [v. 12]; 'This sin of the young men was very great in the Lord's sight, for they were treating the Lord's offering with contempt' [v. 17]; 'they slept with the women who served at the entrance to the Tent of Meeting' [v. 22].

How did all this affect Samuel? Surely no one could stand firm and develop spiritual stature under such conditions. But Samuel did, and his

secret lay in three phrases from that same chapter:
'but the boy ministered before the Lord under Eli
the priest' [v. 11]; 'But Samuel was ministering
before the Lord' [v. 18]; 'Meanwhile, the boy
Samuel grew up in the presence of the Lord' [v.
21].

To stand before God develops consistency
and leads to maturity: 'And the boy Samuel
continued to grow in stature and in favour with
the Lord and with men' [v. 26].

Standing before God -
will teach you to be sensitive to God's voice

Unless you hear from God, you have nothing to
give those to whom you are ministering. Hearing
the voice of God is all part of the exercise of
standing daily in His presence. The practice of
seeking the mind of the Lord is a vital biblical
principle.[4]

In 2 Kings 3:11 we read,

> But Jehoshaphat asked, 'Is there no prophet of
> the Lord here, that we may inquire of the Lord
> through him?' An officer of the king of Israel
> answered, 'Elisha son of Shaphat is here. He
> used to pour water on the hands of Elijah.'
> Jehoshaphat said, 'The word of the Lord is with
> him.'

4   I deal with listening to the voice of God more fully
      in Chapter 9

In the old covenant the ability to hear God resided in the prophet. As new covenant people we can all hear God's voice.

If one called to ministry fails to stand before God he will not hear 'the still small voice' [1 Kings 19:12 RSV]; instead he will be dominated by other voices: the voice of reason, of compromise, of self-protection, or even the voice of the people. Each of these will vie for his attention.

Standing before God -
is the place of intercession and faith

What do you do when you are faced with an impossible situation? That is what confronted Abraham. He had already taken a great step of faith when he was told that Sarah was to have a child. Then the Lord told him that He was going to examine the state of Sodom and Gomorrah because of its great sinfulness. Abraham knew the situation already and it was grim. The men who had brought the good news that Sarah was going to conceive a child were already on their way to Sodom. What should Abraham do? Should he hurry to Sodom and try to preach a message of righteousness to the people? Should he discuss the situation with Lot? He did neither of these: 'but Abraham remained standing before the Lord' [Genesis 18:22].

The leader who stands before God in dependence upon Him is a man of prayer and of faith. If a prayer meeting has been replaced by a committee meeting, the wrong gathering has been cancelled. It is amazing to witness reactions to the suggestion that a church council or meeting of deacons should spend its entire meeting in prayer. Have you ever given a leadership meeting entirely over to prayer?

We recently needed to make a very important decision which would vitally effect the future development of our Church. A meeting had been arranged so that we could arrive at a decision. As the time approached for the meeting, I became increasingly uneasy. I knew that it would be easy to arrive at a human verdict as a result of our deliberations. But this was not a moment for talk but for prayer, not the point for human action but for divine intervention. I quickly circulated a memo to all involved to ask them simply to pray and listen. As the reports came back to me from the various folk, I was very aware that God was acting on our behalf.

When God does it, it's easy. I am not trying to say that there is never any need to discuss or talk through situations, but unless the priority of prayer is uppermost, our solutions will be born out of human reason and not God's wisdom.

When leaders have learned to take everything to the throne of God in prayer, they will then be able to lead their people to do the same.

Abraham did not receive the answer he wanted to his prayer, but he knew that his security lay in trusting God. The story ends with these words: 'When the Lord had finished speaking with Abraham, he left, and Abraham returned home' [Genesis 18:33].

Standing before God -
is the basis of boldness and confidence

There have been many times when I have received an invitation to preach or to take a conference which has found me feeling totally inadequate. I could refuse the invitation or struggle on in my own strength.

A couple of years ago I was invited to address a gathering of bankers and business consultants in Germany. After prayer, I accepted the invitation, but as the time drew near became very fearful that I would fail to do the job properly. Quite contrary to my normal method of preparation, I carefully wrote out my message. I had spent hours preparing, yet when I looked at the text I was convicted of my lack of faith, tore up the script and set to prayer. After a very short time God placed a verse of Scripture in my mind, gave me the substance of what needed to be said and the boldness to deliver it.

Self-confidence, a natural human quality, is of doubtful value in terms of spiritual leadership. The danger is that your actions will be confined within its boundaries: when confidence is strong it will tend towards pride and arrogance; if it is weak it will be ruled by fear.

When you work with the confidence that comes from God, you are acknowledging that human actions cannot produce divine results. You stop dispensing human wisdom and start bringing the wisdom that comes from God. You stop withdrawing through fear and begin to step out in faith. You stop taking credit for the work God does through you and make sure all the glory is given to Him.

To stand before God, to listen to His voice, to seek to please Him first and foremost, will develop this kind of confidence and authority.

In ministry there are constant pressures, and therefore you will need to guard against becoming trapped at the centre of opposing forces. Paul was conscious of such forces when he wrote: 'Am I now trying to win the approval of men, or of God? Or am I trying to please men? If I were still trying to please men, I would not be a servant of Christ' [Galatians 1:10].

If you really desire that each person should grow into full maturity in Christ, you will have boldness to bring God's word fearlessly into their lives. This does not mean that you will be harsh and abrasive. Thorough reading of Paul's letters clearly shows that the apostle was full of love and compassion. But because of his awareness of the holiness of God, which demands the highest standards, and of the grace of God, which reaches the depth of human need, he was able to lead his people towards 'the measure of the stature of the fullness of Christ' [Ephesians 4:13 AV].

The Practice of Standing before God

1.   Give time, as you meet with God each day, to be quiet in His presence and listen to His voice.

2.   Make prayer the priority and foundation upon which your ministry is built.

2.   Remember it is God's kindness that leads you towards repentance. Whatever He reveals is always for your good; there is no situation He is unable to redeem.

3.   Do you believe that more is achieved by your activity than by your prayer?

4.   Do you lack boldness and authority in your ministry? Then you need to spend more time standing before God.

SCRIPTURAL AUTHORITY

'But speak the word only, and my servants shall be healed. For I am a man under authority, having soldiers under me.' [Matthew 8:8-9 AV]

A WORD FROM THE HEART

Jesus had authority in his ministry because He was in complete submission to His Father.

Chapter 5

Under God's Authority

I have never thought of myself as being a rebel. I was brought up in a respectable, Christian, middle-class family, did not run riot when I was a teenager, never was in trouble with the police, always considered myself to be even tempered and user-friendly.

It was not until I became part of the ministry centre under Colin Urquhart, where we lived a community life-style and had a clear leadership and authority structure, that I discovered the true state of my heart.

Was I grappling with the 'rule of life' of a bunch of religious nuts, or were there deeper principles that I needed to get to grips with?

Because of my past experience and calling from God, I was soon involved in the leadership with Colin and others. I quickly learned, not only what it was to share in leading the community, but also what it was to submit my life to other people. I had not realized how independent I was until I saw what true submission really meant. Not a slavish obedience to one or two others, but a real trusting relationship where we committed ourselves to lives of mutual submission.

I do not believe that it is possible to claim to be truly living in submission to God's authority unless this has a practical outworking in the context of the body of Christ. I have found that living thus, in submission to other men of God and functioning under their authority, has been one of the most liberating and enabling things in the whole of my Christian life.

A full understanding of this principle came to me in two ways; first through getting to grips with the encounter Jesus had with the Centurion. The account in the gospels was very familiar, but I had always thought it should be 'a man with authority', not 'a man under authority'. The King James translators must have made a mistake. Every time I used to read the story of the healing of the centurion's servant in Matthew 8 the phrase jarred on me and I mentally changed the word. It took many years before I realized that I was wrong, not the translators!

The centurion had seen a quality in the ministry of Jesus that he recognized. He saw that when Jesus spoke, there was a greater power operating through Him than could be accounted for by mere human influence. He saw beyond Jesus to the power of God. This was not difficult for him to understand, for he was in a similar position with regard to the power of Rome.

When the centurion spoke to the soldiers under his command, they knew that the whole authority of the Roman Empire was behind him. So when he said to Jesus: 'But speak the word only, and my servants shall be healed. For I am a man under authority, having soldiers under me' [Matthew 8:8-9 AV], he acknowledged the authority behind Jesus, who responded with astonishment: 'I say unto you, I have not found so great faith, no, not in Israel' [v. 10]. Up to that point, He had not found anyone who so simply and clearly had received an understanding of His authority. The centurion had seen someone who was subject to a greater authority.

Because Jesus was in submission to that authority, He gained all its power and stature. Jesus himself spoke of this in John 5:19 when He said, 'I tell you the truth, the Son can do nothing by himself; he can do only what he sees his Father doing, because whatever the Father does the Son also does.' And later on in the same chapter: 'By myself I can do nothing ... for I seek not to please myself but him who sent me' [v. 30].

Jesus had authority in His ministry because He was in complete submission to His Father. The writer to the Hebrews sums it up like this: 'During the days of Jesus' life on earth, he offered up prayers and petitions with loud cries and tears to the one who could save him from death, and he was heard because of his reverent submission' [ch. 5:7]. *Only when you are under the authority of God can you exercise the authority of His kingdom.*

True authority will be recognized by a willingness in others to submit. We need to note the difference between authority and authoritarianism. Spiritual authority will glorify God, authoritarianism will merely elevate man. Godly authority will release people into liberty, joy, and fruitfulness; human authoritarianism will bring heaviness and legalism.

Paul said: 'Submit to one another out of reverence for Christ' [Ephesians 5:21]. Real spiritual authority cannot work unless each person lives in willing, joyful submission. That is why Jesus said: 'The greatest among you should be like the youngest, and the one who rules like the one who serves' [Luke 22:26].

The leader should be the most submitted person in the whole church. Submitted to God, to His word, to his fellow leaders and to the people. Jesus said: 'But I am among you as one who serves' [Luke 22:27].

A Course on Evangelism

The second way I learnt about being under God's authority came about almost by accident, as I was preparing a course on evangelism.

As I sat down to explore my subject, I opened my Bible at Genesis 1 and noticed the way God had planned that His creation should live and how it had all been spoiled through man's fall. However, what I found most exciting was the way God guided me to set out what He had shown. It is on the next page.

Colossians 1:19-20: 'For God was pleased to have all his fullness dwell in him, and through him to reconcile to himself all things, whether things on earth or things in heaven, by making peace through his blood, shed on the cross.'

The table clearly shows the perfection of God's creation, the effects of man's fall and the significance of the cross in redeeming mankind. It also demonstrates powerfully the whole principle of God's authority and the consequences of operating in independence.

I saw how God had brought order and peace into all that He had created. It began with God who had all authority, sovereignty and power. He brought creation into being by His word and the culmination of that creation was mankind, formed in His own likeness. God gave man dominion because he was under God's authority. Man lived in peace, with order in his life, in the Garden of Eden – the place of God's providing. There was no sin and so man lived in freedom and perfect righteousness, and was protected from all danger. This combination of factors brought about a situation of unity, love and total wholeness. Until sin entered the picture!

A LIFE LIVED UNDER GOD'S AUTHORITY	A LIFE RULED BY THE POWER OF THE ENEMY
GOD	SATAN
Authority-Sovereignty-Power	Sin
Creation	
Man	
Dependence	Independence
Obedience	Disobedience
Submission	Rebellion
Peace	Fear
Order	Disorder
Direction	Confusion
Authority	Dissension
Righteousness	Self-righteousness
Protection	Danger
Unity	Disunity
Love	Hatred
Wholeness	Sickness

Hebrews 2:8

The strategy of the serpent's temptation was to appeal to pride and to precipitate an independent action. 'Did God really say...?' [Genesis 3:1]. That first sin was not only an act of disobedience, but also one of independence: make up your own mind; do your own thing. The result was that Adam and Eve ended up in rebellion against God and had to be banished from the Garden.

The consequence for them, and for all mankind since, has been lives that are dominated by fear, disorder, confusion, dissension, self-righteousness and frustration, to name but a few of the fruits of sin. This has placed man at variance with God and caused him to live with danger, disunity, hatred and sickness as a constant peril.

When man sinned he came out from under the authority of God and therefore lost his peace, order and protection. It is only when a man turns to God in repentance and faith that he comes back under his covering. I realized that, even as a Christian, if I fell to the temptation of independence and disobedience, my life could again be dominated by fear and confusion.

This truth was dynamic. I saw the way in which it related, not only to my course on evangelism, but to the whole matter of authority. Not only was I working out in practice the benefits of my life being under authority, but I was also understanding how essential it was to live in

God's order. I had often heard teaching on how God hated independence and was only content with lives that were lived in complete submission to Him. I now grasped that truth for myself.

Living with a flawed philosophy

Through the domination of humanism, we are living in a society where the very suggestion that we need to live under any external human control is despised. In home life, children are not being disciplined or being given a moral framework. The basic infrastructure of our community is breaking down with crime and violence escalating, as rebellion becomes rampant. Even our Churches are being subjected to one split after another as our rebellious independence reaches epidemic proportions. Most tragically, because God's people have been infected by the 'spirit of the age', their lives are condemned to weakness and mediocrity. We cry out, 'Whatever happened to the power of God?' but do not realise that our unsubmitted heart is at the root of our problem.

We desperately need to be people whose lives are:

- submitted to God,
- submitted to the authority of His Word
- in submitted relationships within the body of Christ, the Church.

The 'lone ranger' Christian is a menace to other believers and a danger to themselves.

Several years ago, I had a situation where I was seeking to bring guidance and correction to a lady in my Church. She was not finding my leadership very easy to receive. I had refused to endorse her plans for a meeting that she was, quite independently, seeking to organize. She reluctantly agreed to postpone her plans. It was her final riposte which disturbed me the most, 'I want you to know that I am 100% committed to this Church, but 101% committed to God.'

I believe that to be in total contradiction to the teaching of scripture. The sad fact is that the pursuance of this philosophy has led this lady to tragic breakdown in her marriage and total isolation from the body of Christ.

> Jesus said, 'Not everyone who says to me, "Lord, Lord," will enter the kingdom of heaven, but only he who does the will of my Father who is in heaven. Many will say to me on that day, "Lord, Lord, did we not prophesy in your name, and in your name drive out demons and perform many miracles?" Then I will tell them plainly, "I never knew you. Away from me, you evildoers!" ' [Matthew 7:21-2].

These people are described as 'evildoers' which means 'workers of lawlessness' in the original language. The fact that their acts of power were not operating *under authority* was to have disastrous consequences.

If you are reacting against what you are reading, *you need to seek God* for His mind on this matter. It will come to you as heart revelation from God, which will require a radical re-education of many of the attitudes and practices which have been the warp and weft of your life since childhood.

The fruit of God's authority in your life

If you look back to the table earlier in this chapter you will see the consequences resulting from, on the one hand, life lived under God's authority, and on the other, life under in influence and control of the enemy. For the truth of the matter is that you cannot be in both places at once. However, it is possible that some areas of life can be in order while other parts are in chaos, although the disorder will usually overwhelm the rest, if it is not checked

However, the blessings of obedience are tremendous, and vital, if you are to know real authority in life and ministry.

I spent fifteen years of my working life in the family business. It was not an easy thing to come into the company as the boss's son. I had status by accident of birth, but respect needed to be won. As more responsibility was given to me by my father, I was allowed an increasing measure of authority. The more I came under his authority, the more authority I could be given. The staff came to realize that when directions and orders came from me, they had the full backing of my father. I could never have more authority than my father, but I could have as much as he had so long as he was willing to give it to me.

Jesus said: 'All authority in heaven and on earth has been given to me. Therefore go and make disciples of all nations' (Mt 28:18-19). The eleven disciples could be given that authority by Jesus because he had received it from his Father.

True authority cannot come by virtue of position in the church. We can vote someone into any office we might wish, but true spiritual authority comes from the relationship a man has with God and the degree of his commitment to the body of Christ.

In Ephesians 4 we read that the result of the work of apostles, prophets, evangelists, pastors and teachers was 'so that the body of Christ may be built up until we all reach unity in the faith and in the knowledge of the Son of God and become mature, attaining to the whole measure of the fullness of Christ' [v. 12-13].

The questions we may ask concerning people under our care are as follows:

- Are they becoming mature in Christ?
- Is order coming into their lives?
- Do we all have a common purpose?

• Is there growth and fruitfulness?

If these things are not happening as they should, it may be because of a lack of authority in leadership.

Too tough or too friendly?

The word "authority" can have very heavy overtones and seem to indicate someone who is tough and overbearing. On the other hand it may be considered that too much close contact with those you are leading will weaken your position, and produce 'familiarity that breeds contempt'.

It is possible for those who exercise authority in the Church to become aloof and remote from the people. However, is this inevitable, or is it possible to be open, vulnerable and friendly without loosing stature and effectiveness?

I do believe that a leader should be available and touchable. Jesus was called "the friend of sinners"; and when addressing His disciples He said, "You are my friends..." I believe it is important to develop friendship with those you are leading, although it is fully understood that you cannot have a close and deep friendship with everyone in a large Church. This fact is often the cause of tension, particularly as a Church grows and as the leader has added responsibilities.

You do however need a number of close relationships, because people need to get to know you as a real person, not simply as an authority figure. It is also important to be accountable and have those around you who can advise you when you seem to be making wrong decisions. Also, because your authority is a reflection of a living relationship with God, the people need to experience this at close quarters. It is vital to listen to the people whom God has called you to lead and hear what they are saying; not because you are trying to please them instead of God, but because you need to be aware at first hand of the effect of your leadership.

Sharing thoughts, hopes, and aspirations openly will help the people share your vision. They will more readily buy into the vision and identify with it as belonging to them. This does not mean that you simply offload all your problems and dilemmas. There is a loneliness in leadership that is an inevitable part of your calling from God. There are decisions that you have to make and directions that you will give; these can only come out of seeking the will of God in the secret place.

A leader needs to learn that the only person who can carry his burden is the Lord. "Cast your cares on the Lord and he will sustain you; He will never let the righteous fall." [Psalm 55:22] If you are looking to people to give you strength instead of God, you will be disappointed and your authority will be weakened.

There is an old image of the vicar as one who lived in a large house at the end of a long drive, and stood six feet above contradiction on Sundays. The modern image of the Christian guru, is of one who stays in a large hotel, drives around in a stretch limo and is constantly surrounded by bodyguards. But the apostle John did not find Jesus so difficult to reach, he said, "That which we have heard, which we have seen with our eyes, which we have looked at and our hands have touched – this we proclaim." [1 John 1:1]

Being under God's authority will not make you unreachable; in fact the more you enter into a depth of relationship with God, the more like Jesus you will be.

God's authority brings unity

> My prayer is not for them alone. I pray also for those who will believe in me through their message, that all of them may be one, Father, just as you are in me and I am in you. [John 17:20-21]

We can know unity in the church if we will simply follow the teachings of Jesus and some basic scriptural principles.

1.   God calls His people together to be an expression of His body in the place where He has put them.

2.   God raises up leaders among them to hear His voice and to direct His people.

3.   Principles of truth and life are given to the body of Christ to guide it into growth and fruitfulness.

Unity begins with hearts that meet at the cross of Jesus. Unity grows as hearts are bound together in loving relationship. Unity gathers strength as leaders commit themselves to one another and listen to God's direction together. 'Submit to one another out of reverence for Christ' [Ephesians 5:21]. The outcome of unity is God's blessing: 'For there the Lord bestows his blessing, even life for evermore' [Psalm 133:3].

We have a choice: we can argue that because of all the failures of history we are justified in living in disunity today; or we can receive the promises of God and work out the reality of living in unity today. It all stems from a living relationship with God and a loving commitment to Christ's body.

I live in unity with my wife Joyce. That does not mean that we always agree about everything, but because our love and commitment are so deep we work through our difficulties and make sure we arrive at harmonious solutions. So it should be with God's people.

Peace is not the absence of turmoil; it is to know that God is in control despite the circumstances. Jesus demonstrated that peace throughout His life. He was never hassled. He never manifested worry or anxiety. He could therefore say to His disciples: 'Peace I leave with you; my peace I give you. I do not give to you as the world gives. Do not let your hearts be troubled and do not be afraid' [John 14:27]. Paul described this as 'the peace of God which transcends all understanding' [Philippians 4:7]. A peace that is not of human origin is a mark of one under authority. Our strife-torn world is crying out for this quality of peace. However, you will only be able to liberate others into God's peace when you have received it for yourself.

Applying God's Authority to Life and Ministry

1. First, examine your life in relation to God. Are you submitted to God, or are you blaming Him for the difficulties in your life?

2. Now, examine your life in relation to the Bible. Is it your rule of life, or are you constantly arguing with its message?

3. Do you live a submitted life in your family?

4. What is your relationship to your Church? If you are the leader, are you recognized as one who lives in submitted relationship with your fellow leaders and the people?

SCRIPTURAL AUTHORITY

Therefore confess your sins to each other and pray for each other so that you may be healed.
[James 5.16]

A WORD FROM THE HEART

And when is God likely to send an extraordinary work? At a time of extraordinary need when His people are in the grip of an extraordinary desire and when nothing short of an extraordinary outpouring of the Holy Spirit will satisfy.

Chapter 6

Revival and the Power of God

I have always had a passion for revival and an insatiable appetite for books about past revivals. Cornwall, my native county, has had its share of these. John Wesley had a very powerful effect on the county, spawning hundreds of chapels which still stand as monuments to past glory. Billy Bray was another famous Cornishman who moved in revival power. My favourite character however is William Haslam, an Anglican minister and contemporary of Billy Bray, who was converted whilst preaching in his own church at Baldhu, near Truro, and prompted an immediate outbreak of revival.

Revival is an overworked word, which I find myself reluctant to use in this book; however, it is a dynamic that is essential in the life of every leader. Revival is that condition where God is constantly at work in my life maintaining me in a state of usefulness. It indicates that I am willing to be totally open before God and man concerning my sin and weakness – not so that my inadequacy is displayed to others, but because it is part of a process of change. It also shows that I am constantly available for more of God's convicting power to be at work in me, while I seek to be a channel through whom God can pour out His miracle power into the lives of others. The operation of personal revival in the heart of a leader is part of a process of releasing greater power and authority in life and ministry.

A good honest look at yourself

There are two contrasting elements to the work of revival; the one is deliberate and analytical, the other dynamic and subjective.

Charles Finney, trained as a lawyer, lived in the USA in the last century, and saw God move in revival power for more than 30 years. He wrote a definitive work on Revival in which he outlined its major hindrances. At the time when God began a work of revival in my life, I was introduced to this personal check-list entitled, 'Preparing for Revival', which had been condensed from Finney's book[5], and which I nicknamed *The Finney List*. It was somewhat daunting, and began thus:

5   *Finney on Revival*, Dimension Books, Bethany Fellowship

- ❧ Examine your heart concerning wrong relationships and attitudes towards others;
- ❧ dissension towards those in authority;
- ❧ jealousy;
- ❧ speaking evil of others;
- ❧ worldliness; secret sins;
- ❧ laxity in spiritual discipline;
- ❧ unreliability;
- ❧ hardness of heart (especially towards God's word);
- ❧ unholiness;
- ❧ lack of openness towards others …

The list continued with further hindrances:

- ❧ a lack of gratitude and love towards God;
- ❧ neglect of the Bible, prayer, family responsibilities;
- ❧ lack of watchfulness over oneself and one's brethren;
- ❧ neglect of self-denial and the means of grace.

Other stumbling blocks were

- ❧ unbelief;
- ❧ pride;
- ❧ envy;
- ❧ slander;
- ❧ levity;
- ❧ lying;
- ❧ cheating;
- ❧ hypocrisy;
- ❧ robbing God;
- ❧ bad temper;
- ❧ plus hindering others from being useful.

This list helped me to search my heart and come to God in repentance. It was not intended to crush or condemn, but to bring a fresh liberty as my life was laid before God to a greater depth than ever before.

This enabled me to clearly understand that revival does not fall out of the sky like a bolt of lightning, but comes to those who are seriously seeking God and are prepared to be dealt with by Him. Later I was to read accounts of past revivals and discovered that at the centre of every sovereign awakening of God were people who were resolutely seeking Him.

The first time I used this *Finney List* was during a holiday in Scotland, when we were staying on an isolated croft in the Western Highlands. This was during the time when we were living at the Hyde, and God had begun to deal with us in a new and deep way. It was Easter and we were taking a short break with our children. Despite the fact that we were on holiday, Joyce and I realized that our priority was to seek God. We therefore arose early, made a cup of coffee and went out to the cliff top to pray.

As the sun rose and shed its early morning light on the Isle of Skye and the Cuillins, we worked our way steadily through the list, a few things each day. We did not set out to expose one another's sin, but concentrated on our own. Each spoke out the things that God was saying and then prayed them through.

It was one of the loveliest holidays we have ever had. We were blessed with six days of sunshine which aided our relaxation and fun and, with God at work in the way He was, it also became one of the holiest holidays we have ever spent!

The initial preparation for revival is to allow God to reveal sin in your life by His Holy Spirit. Conviction of sin should then lead to confession. That is what was happening on the cliff top in Scotland. God was putting His finger on one area after another which we were confessing to God and to each another.

We began to understand in a new way the truth of the words: 'Therefore confess your sins to each other and pray for each other so that you may be healed' [James 5:16]. That brought a new depth of understanding into our marriage and released the cleansing of God into our lives. As John writes: 'If we confess our sins, he is faithful and just and will forgive us our sins and purify us from all unrighteousness' [1 John 1:9]. As God meets with you in His holiness there will always be conviction, confession and cleansing. This is an important preparation.

But true revival goes deeper than that. Conviction needs to lead to repentance. Repentance precedes brokenness and radical change. It is possible to confess the same sin over and over again. Each time God is faithful and will forgive and cleanse you; but saying 'sorry' is not repentance. Repentance involves not only confession with regard to sin, but a change of will which is expressed in altered behaviour. Your will is thus set in line with God's will.

True repentance leads to brokenness. Brokenness is a word that is much misunderstood. Many people think that it is to be so demoralized before God that you collapse in a heap of discouragement. That is not true! Brokenness deals with selfishness and pride, so that the life of Jesus can be liberated within you. In fact, it might be a better concept to describe brokenness as a willingness to be moulded, as a potter moulds clay. The clay needs to remain wet and supple so that the potter has full liberty to create whatever he wills.

Roy Hession put it like this in *The Calvary Road*:

> To be broken is the beginning of revival. It is painful, it is humiliating, but it is the only way. It is being 'not I, but Christ', and a 'C' is a bent 'I'. The Lord Jesus cannot live in us fully and reveal Himself through us until the proud self within us is broken. This simply means that the hard, unyielding self, which justifies itself, wants its own way, stands up for its rights, and seeks its own glory, at last bows its head to God's will, admits its wrong, gives up its own way to Jesus, surrenders its rights, and discards its own glory - that the Lord Jesus might have

all and be all. In other words, it is dying to self and self-attitudes.[6]

Time spent in deliberately opening up to God's searchlight was to become a vital part of the Leaders' Weeks at the Hyde. Early on in the week I would hand out the *Finney Lists* to each person and encourage them to find a quiet place where they could go through the checklist in the presence of God. This proved to be a powerfully creative exercise. It is however only one side of the deep workings of God in our lives.

This deliberate exercise of self-examination and reflection is not a one-off activity, but something which is important to repeat at regular intervals. It is like a spiritual spring clean.

In the holy presence of God

The second way in which we encounter God is dynamic and subjective, and happens as time is spent in His holy and powerful presence. This is how God dealt with me as I first encountered Him in His revival power. We had given time to seeking Him and working through the personal check-list during our holiday in Scotland. Repentance had brought a new release of the Spirit's power. But we knew that there must be something more to revival than we had yet

6   Roy Hession, *The Calvary Road*, CLC 1950

experienced. As we returned to the fellowship from our Easter break, Colin began to teach about holiness at our daily morning prayer times. It was amazing how we had overlooked the scriptural teaching about holiness.

> Make every effort to live in peace with all men and to be holy; without holiness no-one will see the Lord. [Hebrews 12:14]

> But just as he who called you is holy, so be holy in all you do; for it is written: 'Be holy, because I am holy'. [1 Peter 1:15-16]

God desires a holy people who are set apart for Him. How can it happen? Is it really possible?

God spoke clearly and directed us to give quality time to being in His presence and seeking to meet with Him in holiness, power and glory. This first encounter with God was strange and new. As we came together, Colin introduced the meeting by saying: 'I have never been in such a gathering as this before and haven't any idea what is going to happen. We have come to meet with God, so let's pray.' This was followed by a simple one-sentence prayer: 'Lord, please come and meet with us in your holiness.'

We began with worship. It was different—not the joyful praise that often happens at the beginning of a meeting, but singing which had a fresh depth and beauty. A prophetic word was spoken out. But the most powerful aspect was the feeling that Jesus was among us in His holiness. His holiness was revealing our unholiness and we began to call out to the Lord for His forgiveness and mercy. Spontaneously there was open confession of sin. To pray sitting down became totally inappropriate as we fell to our knees and faces before God. There was deep conviction and tears. Much of the confession was concerning relationships: forgiveness and reconciliation was happening all around. Time stood still as God brought us through repentance to his peace.

We had just begun to understand those words of David: 'Create in me a pure heart, O God, and renew a steadfast spirit within me.' [Psalm 51:10]

This time of seeking God, which was to span three days, took us steadily and gently deeper into His power and presence. More of the darkness of our hearts was brought into the light and dealt with. As our time drew to a close, we had a tremendous sense of the glory of God among us. We rose to our feet to shout our praises to Him who had so graciously revealed himself to us.

At the time it was difficult for others to understand this encounter with God, unlike today, when so many have experienced the powerful presence of God. Thousands have journeyed to the Airport Church in Toronto, others have visited Churches in this country where the presence of God has been poured out, and for many others God has been at work in their own local Church.

I believe it is important to seek to understand what was happening as God dealt with us at that time, and to see what principles were involved. I see that there were three components to God's work among us.

First, there was what Finney would call 'breaking up the fallow ground'. That began with *The Finney List*. Deliberate and thorough repentance was a vital prelude to the revival that was to follow.

Secondly, there was anointed teaching from God's word. It covered many areas including holiness and the renewing of our minds. It produced more repentance and was very fruitful. The scriptures will always bring knowledge so that experience does not become an end in itself. Power without knowledge can be very destructive. If all the power of an aircraft jet engine is unleashed without being attached to an appropriately designed aircraft the result is disaster. Rolls-Royce produce some of the most powerful aero engines in the world, which when built into the latest European Airbus, create one of the most efficient means of transport yet invented. Power and knowledge have worked together. They are not at variance with each other, both are vital for success.

But thirdly, there were the days of seeking God, when the repentance lists and the teaching were laid aside and we came together in the presence of God. By his Spirit He was able to uncover things that would never have been revealed through *Finney's list* and the teaching alone. But time had to be found, even if it was sacrificial and costly, in which we made sure we really did seek the Lord's face in a new way. Not only was sin revealed but power was released.

These principles were later to become vital components of the Leaders' Weeks. There was teaching from the word, time was given for searching hearts with the *Finney list*, but most important, time was spent in God's holy presence. All these things could be done alone, but it was a great blessing to seek God with others who had the same desire.

This has transformed the character of our prayer meetings ever since and is the foundational principle in our prayer meetings at Living Waters Church. In earlier times, prayer meetings were centred on intercession and time was spent asking God to act in the various situations around. Now our Prayer Meeting is primarily a time for seeking God. I will sometimes find that God gives me a starting point, but most of the time as we begin to worship the Lord He will reveal Himself to our hearts and lead us to seek Him afresh. Through this God deals with our hearts, reveals His greatness and sharpens our focus in ministry.

Walking in the light of God

No one told us that when God revealed himself to us in His holiness we would find ourselves confessing our sins to each other. We later read that it was a feature of revivals throughout history. If we had known this, some of us may not have been so eager to meet with Him!

Why does this happen? It is because God is light and when invited to come among His people, He not only comes as the holy God but also as the light. His light exposes the darkness of our hearts. 'But if we walk in the light, as he is in the light, we have fellowship with one another, and the blood of Jesus, his Son, purifies us from every sin.' [1 John 1:7]

This had a powerful effect upon our personal relationships within the fellowship. We realized that if our lives were to be clear and open channels for the power and authority of God, we needed to live in peace and harmony with one another. One morning this principle was tested in a rather embarrassing and unusual way.

Leaders' Weeks always placed a strain upon the family; there was a very heavy schedule from early morning till late at night. It would have been easier in many ways if it had not taken place at my home base, and I sought to minimise the disruption to the family by being with them at all meal times.

One particular Wednesday, I was on my way to the breakfast table when I diverted into the family room and flicked on the television to find out the latest news on the Commonwealth Games, which were taking place in Australia. I have always taken a keen interest in athletics. To my surprise, I had switched on at the beginning of the 5000 metres race in which Brendon Foster was running. He was one of the few athletes in the Great Britain team who had a real chance of winning. Immediately I was captivated; ignoring the call to breakfast, I continued to watch to the end, and by the time I arrived in the dining room the children were leaving the house for school. One look at Joyce's face was enough to reveal that my broken promise had not gone un-noticed. A few cross words were exchanged, but the situation remained unresolved.

Before we were able to remedy the position, I had to leave the house to pray with my team, before the start of the day's programme. I knew I had blown it, and asked God for His forgiveness, knowing that I would need to seek Joyce's forgiveness later, as well as that of my children.

The first meeting of the day was always set aside for Revival Prayer and Seeking God; which Joyce sometimes attended, family responsibilities permitting. I was not really expecting her after our earlier upset; however, to my surprise and horror, just as we had begun the time of worship and praise, in walked Joyce! What was I going to do? The whole purpose of the meeting was to spend time in openness and honesty in God's presence and to seek Him, and I was leading the meeting!

The singing reached a natural break point, which was normally the place where I would have encouraged everyone to be open to God and to respond in confession or repentance. Now, my lips were sealed. What could I say? What would all these leaders think of me if I were to deal with my domestic quarrel in public? But where would my integrity be if I failed to practise what I preached?

I knew there was only one possible course of action. Looking over to where Joyce was sitting, I said, 'Joyce, will you please forgive me for watching the television this morning and missing breakfast with the family?' The atmosphere was electric. Her response was immediate, 'I do forgive you.' I continued with a few more words of explanation and wondered what effect this revelation would have on the meeting. What followed was remarkable. The openness and spontaneity of the people was amazing. God broke into the room and met with everyone. Somehow or other, the fact that Joyce and I had been willing to deal with this situation so frankly and openly, had broken through. I know that we could not have done otherwise, and have truly claimed to walk constantly in God's light.

The light of God's presence exposes darkness and causes hearts to cry out in confession and repentance. True fellowship with God is marred if there is any darkness or unconfessed sin. Fear of open confession disappears when the reality of God is greater than the awareness of the people around. It becomes more important to know that I am right with God than that my reputation is preserved before men.

That unresolved situation would not only have spoilt my fellowship with God, but would have affected my relationships with others. So it has become a principle to always confess my sin to anyone who I have offended or hurt, and receive their forgiveness. This is what it means to 'walk in the light'.

There are three elements to walking in the light:

• *It is towards God*

When the light of God's holiness shines into my life and exposes the darkness, my first concern is to get right with God. Therefore, I confess my sin to God and receive His cleansing according to the promise of 1 John 1:9. Walking in the light produces cleansing.

• *It is towards others*

Sin is never private. It will always affect others either directly or indirectly, so I need to confess my sin to the ones who have been touched by it. That is the James 5:16 principle: 'Therefore confess your sins to each other and pray for each other so that you may be healed.' Walking in the light produces healing of relationships, hurts and misunderstanding; reconciliation where sin has divided; restoration where sin has caused alienation.

- *It defeats Satan.*

Confession with the mouth is very powerful.

A Moment of Crisis

Here is another personal example. Shortly after this first powerful encounter with God, whilst out on the travelling ministry, I suddenly discovered that one of the girls in the team was sexually attracting me in a way that was both disturbing and difficult to understand. It did not seem to have arisen out of my action or hers. Nothing overt was happening between us. My marriage was under no strain and my love for Joyce was continuing to grow and become stronger rather than weaker. No, this seemed to be an attack from the enemy who was trying to bring darkness into my life and to promote sin.

I was puzzling over this, having prayed about it, when it occurred to me that I should have a chat with one of my fellow-leaders. I went to see him in his study one morning and told him the situation, looking for his help. He simply said:

'Now you have walked in the light with me about this you don't need to worry any more. The enemy's power is broken.'

He was right. I walked out of that room a free man. I saw a new depth of meaning in Romans 10:10 – 'For it is with your heart that you believe and are justified, and it is with your mouth that you confess and are saved.' Walking in the light produces victory over temptation and sin; however, just a word of warning: open confession that is too detailed and intimate can do more harm than good. For example, to confess lustful thoughts will cause no problem if described simply by those two words, but any more detail would be harmful to the hearers and would not release any more healing into the life of the person making the confession.

As with the situation just recounted, when the situation is delicate, simply walk in the light with one other person of your own sex. Once I had gained the victory over this temptation I later was able to talk it through with Joyce without it causing her distress.

These principles are particularly important for those who are called to be leaders. The pressure and the potential isolation of leadership produce extreme vulnerability. It is sad to hear of people whose lives and ministries have been destroyed through moral lapses and other areas of sin that

...never have happened had they walked in the
... with just one other person.

It is important that a leader is really open and
ready to walk in the light with others. Your
openness will release openness in others. As you
make walking in the light a principle of your life,
those you lead will quickly follow—that is, if they
are serious about God and want to live in His
revival power.

Revival releases greater authority

A leader who has met with God in his revival
power and through brokenness found the
repentance that leads him to the foot of the cross,
will receive cleansing and experience a fresh
anointing of God's power through His Holy
Spirit. God will then be in His rightful place at
the centre of the leader's life and work, and the
leader will be in his right place before God.
Revival is an antidote to pride in leadership, and
releases prayer and faith in the people.

- In revival, God shows you His view of
  your sin and leads you to repentance.
- In revival, God shows you His view of
  your life and leads you to holiness.
- In revival, God shows you His view of
  other Christians and leads you into new
  relationships of love and living in the
  light with one another.

• In revival, God shows you His view of the world and leads you into a new heart compassion for the lost.

Does this then mean that when God sends a mighty spiritual awakening through the nation (as He did in Wesley's day) that it will necessarily be through those who are actively seeking His revival power? It may be, or it may not: God is sovereign. But it is certainly true that God's revived people are instruments He can use to promote such an awakening, and equally true that His people's disobedience and unbelief can delay or even prevent revival.

I can identify with many things that have happened in past revivals, but there are other manifestations of God's power that I have not yet seen. I long to see God move in Holy Spirit fire in this land as He did in bygone days.

I will conclude this chapter with a quotation from Richard Owen Roberts's book on Revival which beautifully sums up that longing for a greater outpouring of revival:

When can revival be expected? If revival is the extraordinary movement of the Holy Spirit, it can be expected when the sovereign God of the universe sends it. And when is God likely to send an extraordinary work? At a time of extraordinary need when His people are in the grip of an extraordinary desire and when nothing short of an extraordinary outpouring of the Holy Spirit will satisfy.[7]

7   Richard Owen Roberts, *Revival,* Tyndale Hse 1982

Living in Revival

1. Set aside time to work through the *Finney List*. Do not allow it to bring condemnation, don't hurry, and act upon everything that God shows you.

2. Get together with other like-minded people for a time of seeking God. You might find it helpful to attend a conference which is devoted to seeking God.

3. Keep short accounts with God, don't let sin blunt your effectiveness. Learn to make 'Walking in the light' a principle of life.

4. Beware of danger points where wrong relationships and unresolved conflicts could trip you up.

SCRIPTURAL AUTHORITY

So then death is at work in us, but life is at work in you.
[2 Corinthians 4:12]

A WORD FROM THE HEART

In coming to Christ we do not bring our old life up onto a higher plane; we leave it at the cross. The corn of wheat must fall into the ground and die
[A. W. Tozer, *The Alliance Witness*, 1946]

Chapter 7

I have been Crucified with Christ

The prophetic word that changed the whole course of my life included these phrases ... 'I am seeking out a people who will bring my message of revival ... the distinguishing characteristic will be that they are indelibly marked with the mark of the cross.'

Jesus said: 'If anyone would come after me, he must deny himself and take up his cross daily and follow me. For whoever wants to save his life will lose it, but whoever loses his life for me will save it.' [Luke 9:23-2]

There is a strange logic in the principle of spiritual authority. The apostle John put it this way, 'He must increase, but I must decrease.' Paul expressed it thus, 'For when I am weak, then I am strong.'

Jesus said, 'Take up your cross daily and follow me.' But what does that really mean? There are those of you who will have seen Arthur Blessit carrying the wooden cross, on video if not in real life, which he did throughout the world to great effect. If you happen to be one of those who saw him, one thing you will have noticed is that the cross was bigger than he was. This physical example has a spiritual analogy which it is not difficult to see. The cross always needs to be bigger than you are. 'Jews demand miraculous signs and Greeks look for wisdom, but we preach Christ crucified; a stumbling block to Jews and foolishness to Gentiles, but to those whom God has called, both Jews and Greeks, Christ the power of God and the wisdom of God.' It is only when you preach Jesus Christ and him crucified, that you have substantial spiritual authority.

The cross is not only the message, but is also the place of constant forgiveness, peace and power. For the burdens of life and the perplexities of ministry, we have not only a place where they can be laid down, but also a place of healing, reconciliation and victory.

Crucified with Christ

Authority will increase the more the cross is at work in my life. When I was a young Christian I got to know Len Moules, a pioneer missionary, and later International Director of WEC (Worldwide Evangelisation Crusade), and he had a powerful influence on me. It was evident that God had done a very deep work in his life. However, it was not until I read his biography *On to the Summit* that I learned the secret. Here is an extract from the book where we see the cross at work in the life of a leader. Len is speaking:[8]

> One morning the father of one of our missionaries, who was staying with us, asked me if I would go with him for an early walk. I thought he wanted to see the dawn on the Himalayan snows. So I took him to a certain point and said, 'That's the first peak that really gets the sun.' He said, 'I haven't come to see the dawn, I've come to chat with you.'

> And I had an anxious feeling down in my stomach that he had something serious to say. He had. We sat down and he asked, 'Len, do you know Galatians 2:20?' Thank God, I did; and I began to recite it: 'I have been crucified with Christ; it is no longer I who live, but Christ who lives in me; and the life I now live in the flesh I live by faith in the Son of God who loved me and gave himself for me.'

> In fact I never completed it, because half way through he stopped me and said, 'Len, I know you can say it, but what do you know of it? I thank you for letting me be with you at this conference, to see you plan on the blackboard where you are going to put your missionaries. That was not Spirit planning, that was human efficiency in the use of your missionaries. It wasn't God-given.

8   Pat Wraight, *On the Summit,* Kingsway/CLC 1981

'Len, I've heard you praying. Oh that I could say it was the Spirit at prayer, but it wasn't. It was you praying with all your human desires, and asking God's blessing on it.

'You have fun at the table. If only I could feel it was Christ rejoicing in your midst, but not from you, Len. You are such a human human, Len, you know nothing of this. Oh, I know that you'd be willing to give your body to be burned, but Len, it is just the energy of the flesh and you're asking God to bless it. You know nothing of this verse of Scripture.'

And he left me.

It wasn't long after, possibly an hour later, that dawn came on the peaks, but that did not exist as far as I was concerned. I was face to face with God on that issue. Thirteen years as a missionary—and if those works had been tested by fire no doubt they would have gone up as wood, hay and stubble. Human plans, human initiative, human ideas – good ideas. What I thought was best, sacrifice and what not, but was it the Lord's will? Was it spiritual decision? I doubt it. I know it wasn't. An hour later I lay down on the mountainside and spread my arms wide and said, 'Lord, I am crucified with you. Oh, I Live. Thank God for strength and a mind and a heart and a will and emotions and love. Thank you, Lord, I live, but not I, but you live through me.

The impact of the cross puts pride to death and enables the resurrection life of Jesus to shine through. Paul expressed it thus, 'For we who are alive are always being given over to death for Jesus' sake, so that his life may be revealed in our mortal body. So then, death is at work in us, but life is at work in you.' [2 Corinthians 4:11-12]

You can be as full of the Holy Spirit as you want to be!

We know that we need to be filled with the Holy Spirit so that more of God's life and power can be released into our hearts and lives. Why then, among those who have been filled with the Holy Spirit, do some people manifest God's power so much more than others? Has anyone stopped to ask how much is being filled? God cannot take up His rule and reign where humanity and sin reign. We must willingly give over each area of our life to God's control. A. W. Tozer has said:

> It may be said without qualification that every man is as holy and as full of the Spirit as he wants to be. He may not be as full as he wishes he were, but he is most certainly as full as he wants to be.[9]

9   *Born after Midnight,* The Best of A W Tozer, Kingsway 1983

On a glorious hot sunny Sunday, whilst we were living at the Hyde, the decision was made to have our Family Worship on the lawn. I was to give a talk, and took advantage of the changed environment. I wanted to illustrate the truth that we are as full of the Holy Spirit as we want to be.

As I stood before the people, I held a large metal jug in my hand (I had deliberately chosen a metal jug so that no one could see inside) and said, 'This jug represents you and me.' In my other hand I held another jug, and there was a large barrel of water nearby. I then proceeded to fill the jug until the water spilled over the sides splashing onto the grass. I explained that this was a picture of what happens when we ask Jesus to fill us with His Holy Spirit. I then asked the question, 'Is the jug full?' The reply was chorused back by all the children, 'Yes!' I then put my hand into the jug and pulled out a stone on which was written the word 'lies' and proceeded to ask, 'Is the jug full?' to which they accurately responded. 'No!' More water was added until the jug overflowed once again, and the questions were repeated. There were stones called 'disobedience', 'compromise' and 'fear', and others as well. The lesson was applied, more water was added and the truth went home to young and old alike. I have since shared that incident many times, and each time the truth has hit home like an arrow. You are as full of the Holy Spirit as you want to be!

The cross is therefore the pathway to power because it is only as the death of Jesus is at work in our lives, dealing with our sinful humanity, that God is able to fill us more fully with His life and power.

You can be crying out to God for more Holy Spirit and wonder why your life remains unaffected. What you need is more cross. Here again is the message of Romans 6 – not only to be dead to sin but to be alive to God in Christ Jesus: 'Therefore do not let sin reign in your mortal body so that you obey its evil desires. Do not offer the parts of your body to sin, as instruments of wickedness, but rather offer yourselves to God, as those who have been brought from death to life; and offer the parts of your body to him as instruments of righteousness.'
[Romans 6:12-13]

Sin robs your life of spiritual power. So does trying to please God in your own strength. In your humanity it is impossible to please God. To use natural resources is to believe that through effort and hard work you can be effective for God. Paul acknowledged the futility of this when he said: 'I know that nothing good lives in me, that is, in my sinful nature' [Romans 7:18]. Jesus had already told his disciples: 'apart from me you can do nothing' [John 15:5]. Therefore, your own striving needs to go to the cross so that you can reach out to receive God's divine strength. It is the exchanged life that is the powerful life. 'I have been crucified with Christ and I no longer live, but Christ lives in me.' [Galatians 2:20]

The Warehouse Floor

If your life is being daily submitted to God's will, and the cross is at work within you, deep and progressive things can be happening of which you may be totally unconscious.

This happened to me. After God had met with us, as I have recounted in the previous chapter, I spent several months travelling extensively with Colin Urquhart, conducting missions in various centres around the nation. Much of our day was spent in prayer and seeking God. We sought God on our knees in dusty vestries, public halls, carpeted lounges, as well as on the concrete floor of a disused furniture warehouse in Wales. I couldn't count the number of hours we spent on our knees and faces before God that summer. There were times of worship, repentance, seeking God and intercession, but I couldn't honestly tell you that I was conscious of anything specific happening to me.

The summer ended, autumn came, missions finished, and Colin went to South Africa, leaving me in authority at the home base. It now became my responsibility to lead the morning prayer time and to bring a message from God's word each day. On my first day, I had spent time preparing and had received a word from God, which I duly gave. At the conclusion of my message I simply said, 'You've heard what God is saying to you, let's pray now and respond to God.'

There was a moment of silence, then came the sound of sobbing and tears. I was awe struck. Nothing I had said could account for this response. Prayers of repentance flowed and hearts were melted in the presence of God. What on earth had happened? Death had been at work in me, so that life was able to work in them.

Out of the Ashes

God is never in a hurry; He concentrates more on the preparation of the worker, than on the work. Jesus spent thirty years preparing for a ministry which lasted only three years. Joseph spent thirteen very demanding and perplexing years before he was ready for the task to which he was destined.

Joseph's brothers did not understand the ways of God. Upon the death of their father Jacob, they thought that Joseph would exact revenge upon them for selling him into slavery, but this was his testimony, 'Don't be afraid. Am I in the place of God? You intended to harm me, but God intended it for good to accomplish what is now being done, the saving of many lives.' [Genesis 50:19/20]

The cross is a place of refining in the life of a Christian. All who are called to ministry are longing for God to work more through them. They are constantly yearning for a greater demonstration of the power of God. How does God prepare us for greater power and authority? One of the ways is through God's refining fire. In Malachi 3:3 it says, 'He will sit as a refiner and purifier of silver; he will purify the Levites and refine them like gold.' His fire tests me through pressure, perplexity, and persecution, and what will be the result?

Is God trying to put me through some form of punishment? Not at all. My problems and dilemmas are not unusual happenings or something unique for Christians, they are simply the circumstances of life. Satan would want to make capital out of them and destroy me through them, but as I apply the work of Calvary to my life, God employs them to mature, refine and enable me to become more usable in His hands. The cross is doing a refining work in my life.

A young man, full of zeal for God, who lived in our home for a while after returning from a Discipleship School, was looking for his next step. He was trying to gain acceptance at another Bible School, but was running into a number of obstacles. He was perplexed at the difficulties he was encountering and sought my advice. He did not like the answer I gave him, but it seemed perfectly clear to me why he was having such difficulty. So I told him. 'I don't believe that you need any more Bible training at this stage; at this moment you need some training in *The School of Life*'.

It was summer when I first arrived at The Hyde and admired the large open grates in the drawing-room and the library of that magnificent country house, in which log fires burned during the winter months. I was surprised to find a bed of cold ashes about four inches deep in each grate. My initial reaction was to get a bucket and shovel and remove them. However, I restrained myself, and asked why the ashes remained. I was informed that when burning logs in such a large grate, it is essential if the fire is to have any real warmth to have a deep bed of ashes. As the fire is kindled in the grate, the ashes heat up and increase the warmth that is thrown out into the room.

Later, at a Leaders' Week, the drawing-room fire became a parable. The Lord showed me that the grate with the log fire is a picture of our lives. As each circumstance and trial is encountered and brought to the cross, it is dealt with and becomes like ashes in the bed of our lives. Hurts, disappointments, broken dreams and hard times can all be burned in the fire. Rather than these situations working against us, when they are taken to the cross and burnt up in its fire, their ashes act as a reflector for the fire of God to shine through to others.

Dr J. R. Millar in his book about the life of Joseph says: 'Whole, unbruised, unbroken men are of little use to God'[10] Do not despise the testings or the ashes that result. The principle of the cross is: 'Death is at work in us, but life is at work in you' [2 Corinthians 4:12].

Paula Worth, who is a personal friend and was at one time a member of the Fellowship in Sussex, speaks graphically of the continuing work of the cross in our lives.

---

10   J. R. Millar as quoted in Paul E. Billheimer, *The Mystery of His Providence*, Kingsway Publications 1983

The Reason for the Fire

Within this frail vessel lies
The crucible wherein my faith is tested.
The refiner alone knows how delicate is his task;
The flame must be neither so low that dross remains,
Nor yet so high that the fragile beauty of the crucible
Is shattered for ever in its heat.
And so steadily and gently he applies his fire,
His only motive my purification;
His purpose not wavering,
His eyes fixed on the beauty that he will one day behold ...

Regarding nonetheless my present suffering with
compassion,
The identification of one who has also walked in the fire
And proved that it does not utterly consume,
Even if it should include a Calvary.
As in my fire I cry out to him
And see him walking freely towards me,
I realize afresh that only in the fire
Are my bonds burned away;
And I receive a heart poured through with love,
His love to stand with others in their fire,
Until in that final purity
We stand together at his throne.

The death side of the Cross

The tremendous fact about the Cross is that there are two sides, the death side and the life side. It is very important that we are aware of the power that is at work on both sides of the cross.

Paul said, 'If we have been united with him like this in his death, we will certainly also be united with him in his resurrection.'
[Romans 6:5]

A friend of mine once said, 'I want to have a proper death with Christ, because I want a proper resurrection.' I believe that one of the reasons for weak and inept christians is that they have never been to the cross.

In the next chapter we will look at 'The life side of the Cross.'

Have you been to the cross?

1.   Read through Galatians 2:20:-

      I have been crucified with Christ and I no
      longer live, but Christ lives in me. The life I
      live in the body, I live by faith in the Son of
      God who loved me and gave himself for me.

      Meditate on these words and apply them to
      your life.

2.   Are there stones in your jug (see p.108) that
      need removing, so that more of the Holy
      Spirit can be in evidence in your life?

3.   Jesus told His disciples that they should take
      up the cross daily and follow Him. What
      does that mean in practise?

4.   The fire is the place of purity and where
      hurts, pains, disappointments and
      conflicts can be dealt with.

      Do you have any unresolved conflicts
      that have not been put on the fire?

SCRIPTURAL AUTHORITY

'Silver or gold I do not have, but what I have I give you. In the Name of Jesus Christ of Nazareth, walk!' [Acts 3:6]

A WORD FROM THE HEART

Corrie Ten Boom once said, 'God has taken our sins and has buried them in the depths of the sea, and on the shore he has posted a notice saying: **NO FISHING**'

Chapter 8

The Life side of the Cross

The cross is where Jesus won a complete, irrevocable and eternal victory over sin and all the power of Satan. In the last chapter we saw how the cross deals with our sin, pride and self-sufficiency. We now stand fully identified with the cross, we take up the cross daily, and therefore can now enter fully into the resurrection power and life that flows from the life side of the Cross.

In the very early days of the growth and development of Living Waters Church, I found God urging me strongly to teach from the Bible about righteousness: the fact that we are declared righteous before God, not as a result of good behaviour and righteous deeds, but by faith. For many weeks I could not preach about anything else, every time I wanted to change to something else, God simply pointed me back to righteousness, which I found puzzling. However, as I began to talk with the people, I soon understood the reason. There was something ingrained in their minds and spirits that communicated that righteousness depends on doing right things and following a code of behaviour. It took a long time for me to get through to them that it is entirely by faith.

A failure to receive this truth stunts spiritual growth and maturity. Leaders who fail to grasp it live in a continual state of guilt and condemnation which totally undermines their authority, because it makes spiritual power dependent upon personal performance, not on the victory of Jesus on the cross.

I still meet those who are bound by the shame of sins already forgiven, or live in a state of condemnation because of past failure or a moral lapse. God does not approve of sin, but He does forgive sin; and once forgiven, it is forgotten. That is the power of the cross. Perhaps you've heard this story:

I Can't remember

Some years ago in the far West of the United States rumours spread that a certain Catholic woman was having visions of Jesus. The reports reached the archbishop. He decided to check her out. There is always a fine line between the authentic mystic and the lunatic fringe.

'Is it true ma'am, that you have visions of Jesus?'

'Yes,' the woman replied simply.

'Well, the next time you have a vision, I want you to ask Jesus to tell you the sins that I confessed in my last confession.'

The woman was stunned. 'Did I hear you right, bishop? You actually want me to ask Jesus to tell me the sins of your past?'

'Exactly. Please call me if anything happens.'

Ten days later the woman notified her spiritual leader of a recent apparition. 'Please come,' she said.

Within the hour the archbishop arrived. He trusted eye-to-eye contact. 'You just told me on the telephone that you actually had a vision of Jesus. Did you do what I asked?'

'Yes, bishop, I asked Jesus to tell me the sins you confessed in your last confession.'

The bishop leaned forward with anticipation. His eyes narrowed.

'What did Jesus say?'

She took his hand and gazed deep into his eyes. 'Bishop,' she said, these are his exact words: "I CAN'T REMEMBER."' [11]

Corrie Ten Boom once said, 'God has taken our sins and has buried them in the depths of the

11 *The Ragamuffin Gospel*, B.Manning Scripture Press UK 95 p.113

sea, and on the shore he has posted a notice saying: NO FISHING.'

A pure heart and a clear conscience are essential elements if you are to have spiritual authority. Your standing before God and your authority before people will be undermined by the devil unless you have a thorough revelation that you are righteous in the sight of God. The cross of Jesus has the power to ensure that past sin cannot blight your future.

Still in slavery to sin?

A lack of understanding of the power that is available at the life side of the cross can leave you trapped in a state of bondage and defeat. Paul wrote:

> For we know that our old self was crucified with him so that the body of sin might be done away with, that we should no longer be slaves to sin - because anyone who has died has been freed from sin [Romans 6:6-7]

Not only has the work of the cross achieved forgiveness for sins committed, but it has also won victory over sin itself. The resurrection of Jesus pronounced victory over death and it also declared triumph over the power of sin in fallen humanity.

For years the cross was for me no more than the place where my sins were forgiven. I never understood that I could know victory over the power of sin through the cross, and so I lived in defeat and powerlessness. You see, I had more problems with my flesh than I did with my sin! I knew my sins were forgiven, but I thought that I would have to wait until I was in heaven before I could know victory over my human weakness. When the light dawned, I was thrilled to know that whatever sin may try to drag me down, there is victory for me now! I do not have to wait until beyond the grave.

Paul was writing to Christians when he said: 'Put to death, therefore, whatever belongs to your earthly nature: sexual immorality, impurity, lust, evil desires and greed, which is idolatry' [Colossians 3:5]. You can live in victory over temptation and sin!

The extraordinary truth is that when Jesus died He took my sins to death with Him and *He also took me*, all of me: 'I have been crucified with Christ and I no longer live, but Christ lives in me' [Galatians 2:20]. My self-life has been annihilated with Jesus: 'So you also must consider yourselves dead to sin and alive to God in Christ Jesus.' [Romans 6:11 RSV]

How do you receive this victory? First, recognize those areas of darkness, failure and compromise as sin. Ask God to show you the evil of your sin and to enable you to truly repent – that is, to turn away from it. Bring what He has shown you to the cross and ask God for His forgiveness and cleansing.

Confess in the presence of another Christian: 'Therefore confess your sins to each other and pray for each other so that you may be healed' [James 5:16]. That brings the darkness into God's light and breaks the power of it in your life, as I explained more fully earlier in this book.

Some time ago a minister came to me with a most distressing habit: he was totally addicted to the smell of rubber and had surrounded himself with a vast array of rubber items from Wellington boots to hot-water bottles. Now this habit could not exactly be described as sin, yet for him it was sin, because it was undermining the whole effectiveness of his life and ministry as well as causing him acute embarrassment.

He had come to me for prayer with a genuine desire to be rid of it. He willingly confessed the whole situation before God and man. He received forgiveness and cleansing. But how was he to be free from the addiction?

As we prayed together, I remembered what Paul says in Romans:

> Therefore do not let sin reign in your mortal body so that you obey its evil desires. Do not offer your body to sin as instruments of wickedness, but rather offer yourselves to God ... Don't you know that when you offer yourselves to someone to obey him as slaves, you

are slaves to the one you obey - whether you
are slaves to sin which leads to death, or obedience which leads to righteousness?
[Romans 6:12, 13 & 16]

I then applied this to the distressed minister
sitting opposite. I told him, 'At this moment as
we have taken this habit to the cross, you have
received forgiveness, cleansing and have been
set free from its power. However, it will not stop
the devil tempting you, which is what he will seek
to do. But now you have a choice. You can obey
the voice of temptation or the voice of God. Each
time you obey the voice of God, the voice of the
enemy will get weaker. As you commit yourself
as a slave of righteousness you will see the
complete victory. My prayer today is not a quick
fix, but it is a doorway to victory if you will obey
this scripture.'

The greater your leadership responsibility, the
greater will be the pressures on your life, and it
will be increasingly important for you to know
the daily reality of victory over personal sin and
temptation. You will then be able to lead others
into the knowledge of how to live in victory over
sin.

Jesus lived a victorious life, and through the
cross He provided the way for us to follow in His
steps. 'For we do not have a high priest who is
unable to sympathise with our weaknesses, but
we have one who has been tempted in every way,

just as we are – yet was without sin.' [Hebrews 4:15]

You can stop that, in the Name of Jesus

Satan has been robbed of his power and knows that his final sentence has already been pronounced and will most surely be carried out. Paul reminds us of this in Colossians 2:15: 'And having disarmed the powers and authorities, he made a public spectacle of them, triumphing over them by the cross.'

On the life side of the cross there is complete victory over the power of Satan. God's word gives us the assurance that any evidence of the activity of Satan in the life of someone we meet need not be a cause for fear, for we know that through the triumph of the cross we have the right to victory.

A minister from Scotland, let me call him Graham, came to one of the Leaders' Weeks; he had been going through a time of great darkness and arrived in some considerable distress. I observed him during one of the meetings and could see that he was struggling. At the coffee break I sat down beside him. 'What needs to happen to you, Graham?' I asked.

'I need to be set free from all that has been attacking me,' he replied.

We agreed a time when we could meet and pray.

Graham explained his situation, 'I have to admit that I have been very foolish. I have been overworking for a long time and become physically weak. I know that the root cause has been pride; I was not willing to trust others. I also know that I have become very isolated.' He paused briefly, sank back into the chair and continued, 'At first I thought it was simply depression and weakness; but I realise now that I have opened a door to Satan. There had been times during the night when I felt as though someone was trying to physically strangle me, and when someone tried to pray with me back in Scotland, I even became violent and yet at the same time felt someone was trying to choke me.' He was almost in tears now, he knew the end was near; he then added, 'Be careful when you pray for me because I could be violent.'

'That will not happen today,' I told him. Only the previous day, as I had been praying, God had given me a fresh revelation of the authority He had given to me through the cross, over all the powers of darkness. I knew that I had the right to total victory, and I was not prepared to accept anything less.

I would strongly advise, when confronting the powers of darkness, that you do not minister alone; on this occasion another member of my team joined me to share in the time of ministry.

However, the moment we started to pray for his release Graham started to choke and retch, and began to rise out of his chair as if to hit me. I immediately looked at him, but addressed the powers of darkness. 'You can stop that in the name of Jesus,' I commanded. He immediately slumped back into the chair. We continued to minister until we had the assurance that he had received a complete victory.

In a short while Graham prayed a beautiful prayer; he asked God to forgive him for his foolishness and disobedience, and was set free from all that oppressed him. The whole room was bathed in peace as we reached the place of victory. 'I feel as though a light has been turned on,' he said, as he basked in the freedom and joy that God had given him.

Satan is real and powerful and it is important to recognize with Paul that: 'our struggle is not against flesh and blood, but against the rulers, against the authorities, against the powers of this dark world and against the spiritual forces of evil in the heavenly realms' [Ephesians 6:12].

The power of the Name of Jesus is awesome. It is not only a weapon to be used in ministry, but vital for our daily life. My daughter Joanna had a terrifying experience a few years ago. She and her husband Iain had been helping an ex-offender who had come to their church and made a profession of faith in Jesus. He had come into their home when they were both there and seemed to be making real progress.

One particular day when Joanna was returning from work, she met him outside her house and began chatting in her usual friendly and caring manner. During the conversation he mentioned that he needed to write a cheque to pay Jo and Iain for something they had bought for him, but he had no pen. As Jo retreated into the house to get a pen, he followed. Because they were trying to help him, she did not want to over react to this situation, and so let him come in, sit down at the kitchen table and write the cheque. However, once he had finished he got up, grabbed a kitchen knife and forced Jo into the bedroom. As she stood there, something of all that she had learned over the years rose within her and she shouted out, 'In the Name of Jesus, don't you come one step nearer, drop that knife and go!' The ex-offender looked shocked, stopped, dropped the knife and ran from the house. Jo immediately phoned the police. She also miraculously was able to contact Iain (who in his job as a Crown Prosecutor could have been in any number of places) who came immediately and together they were able to pray and receive healing and the peace of God.

But what I have I give you

There is healing on the life side of the cross, and once again it is a revelation of God's power into our hearts that will release this authority.

The account of the healing of the man at the Gate Beautiful in Jerusalem is well known. Only days before, Peter and John had been discouraged and demoralized, but now Jesus has been raised from the dead, He has ascended to God's throne and the Holy Spirit has exploded into the lives of the 120. Something powerful had happened, and now as Peter and John are confronted with the lame beggar, they boldly say, 'Silver or gold I do not have, but what I have I give you. In the Name of Jesus Christ of Nazareth, walk!'

When asked by the rulers and elders for an explanation, Peter fearlessly declares: 'It is by the name of Jesus Christ of Nazareth, whom you crucified but whom God raised from the dead, that this man stands before you healed' [Acts 4:10].

Recently, Joyce and I were ministering to pastors and leaders in southern Germany. I was teaching on the leadership of Jesus as recorded in John's gospel. During my teaching I spoke of the occasion when Jesus healed the royal official's son. Jesus was in Cana of Galilee, the sick child was in Capernaum and the nobleman begged Jesus to come and heal his son, who was close to death. The gospel record continues:

> Unless you people see miraculous signs and wonders,' Jesus told him, 'you will never believe.' The royal official said, 'Sir, come down before my child dies.' Jesus replied, 'You may go. Your son will live.' The man took Jesus at his word and departed.' [John 4:48-50]

When he reached Capernaum he discovered that at the moment Jesus spoke the child had began to recover.

At the end of the evening as we were ministering to the people, Joyce prayed with a Pastor's wife who was struggling with the whole issue of unbelief because her 4-year-old daughter, after an ear infection, had been left with severely impaired hearing. She and her husband had prayed for healing without seeing any improvement. As Joyce prayed into this situation, God directed her to speak about Thomas's inability to believe without seeing, and so she prayed specifically that this lady would see God at work, which would then restore her faith in the miraculous. She immediately fell to the ground, receiving from the Lord. Joyce was just about to pray for the next person in line when God spoke into her heart, 'Tell that woman, when she reaches home tonight her daughter will be healed.'

For a moment Joyce argued with God, but the words would not go away. So in obedience and faith she spoke to her, through an interpreter, and gave her the clear word from God. The woman's response was, 'It will take me half an hour to drive home, and I am not sure that I can keep my faith alive that long.' Joyce told her to praise the Lord and pray in tongues all the way home. Then the faith battle started in Joyce's mind, 'Was that me, or was it God?' She even woke in the night grappling with the same question; but the Lord's answer was, 'The child is healed.'

The conference was to continue the following morning, and as the people arrived, this lady came through the door with her face wreathed in smiles. She came straight over to Joyce, and said, 'Last night when you gave me that word I was thrilled, and yet could hardly believe it. I did what you said and prayed in tongues all the way home. Just before I went to bed, I took my daughter to the toilet, still praying in tongues. She said to me, 'Stop shouting, Mummy, stop shouting.' It then dawned on me that she could hear, at breakfast she kept on telling the family to stop shouting, and then we knew God had done a miracle.

Hallelujah! What I have I give you! There is healing on the life side of the cross.

The Power that is at work within us

1. Do you know that you are righteous? Is there any guilt or condemnation that is blunting your authority?

2. Is the power of the cross enabling you to live in victory over sin and temptation? Spend time applying the principle of Romans 6:12,13 & 16.

3. The cross is where Jesus inflicted a complete, irrevocable and eternal victory over sin and all the power of Satan.

   Is there any area of your life where the devil has got a foothold? Get rid of him in the Name of Jesus.

4. How strong is your confidence in the name of Jesus?

5. 'What I have I give you.' What do you have, and what are you doing with it?

SCRIPTURAL AUTHORITY

Were not our hearts burning within us while he talked with us on the road and opened the Scriptures to us? [Luke 24:32]

A WORD FROM THE HEART

It is important to realize that when God speaks to you it will most often be with that 'still small voice' and you need time to learn to become sensitive to it.

Chapter 9

Is there any word from the Lord?

Over the many years I have led seminars and retreats for leaders, I have heard a constantly recurring heart cry 'I do not seem to be able to hear God,' which is sometimes put in the form of a question: 'Will you teach me how to hear God?'

The truth is that every Christian can hear God. You cannot become a Christian without having heard God. Jesus said: 'I tell you the truth, whoever hears my word and believes him who sent me has eternal life and will not be condemned; he has crossed over from death to life' [John 5:24]. Every child of God can go back in His mind to the time when God spoke – through a sermon, book, testimony, or in some other way – and he responded to His call and was born again.

Through the call of God you are born into the new life of Jesus. When you are baptized in the Holy Spirit, God plants His voice in you; it is as though a radio receiver is placed within you. Jean Darnall, a pioneer of the move of the Spirit in this country, used to say that the baptism in the Holy

Spirit puts the Spirit of the Seer within you. A Seer is an old fashioned name for a prophet; it is like a pun in the English language because it makes you a 'see-er', enabling you to see things with the eyes of God. His voice is not simply divine insight, but an expression of His love and commitment towards you, for He desires your friendship and fellowship.

God is always speaking

> The heavens declare the glory of God;
> the skies proclaim the work of his hands.
> Day after day they pour forth speech;
> night after night they display knowledge.
> [Psalm 19:1f]

God is constantly trying to communicate with His people, through His creation and in thousands of other ways, but those in leadership need to receive more specific instructions and therefore to tune their ears more acutely to His voice.

It is important to realize that when He speaks to you it will most often be with that 'still small voice' and you need time to learn to become sensitive to it. I can pick out the voice of my wife Joyce in a crowded room, because I have learned to recognize its particular pitch and tone. If you play a musical instrument, say a flute, you can hear its sound even when listening to a full orchestra. It is because your ear is tuned in. Listening to God is like that. We must learn to pick out the sound of His voice in the midst of a noisy world.

Not long after I was filled with the Holy Spirit, I met Eddie Smith, a travelling Bible teacher who had an anointed healing ministry. I was fascinated by the way he prayed for people, particularly in small meetings. His normal practice, after having preached, was to lay hands on every person in the room and begin his prayer in this way, 'O Lord, I am asking you to bless this your child in body, mind and spirit.' After this opening sentence he would pause and listen to God with total confidence that God would show him any definite points of need in any of the three areas he had specified. He would then continue to pray as God directed him.

Joyce and I were fascinated by all this; for at that time we were totally inexperienced in such accurate listening. One evening, we were to test out the genuineness of this amazing style of ministry, for we had invited a very open, yet unbelieving, girl to the meeting, and Joyce was experiencing a distressing and persistent gynaecological problem. Eddie had told us that when he prayed for physical healing he felt the symptoms in his own body, which is one form of the gift of the 'word of knowledge'.

Now we will know whether this is genuine, we thought. We did not have any serious doubt concerning the integrity of Eddie's ministry, but were fascinated to see what God would reveal.

As usual, Eddie preached a word that encouraged faith and then began to pray around the room. When he arrived at our young friend he paused, and began, 'O Lord bless this dear one and bring her to yourself.'

Wow! God had shown him that she needed to give her life to Jesus and receive his salvation. Eddie continued to pray for others and sought God for any specific healing that they might need. We were on the edge of our chairs; how would he cope with Joyce's very delicate situation? When it was her turn for prayer, he began in the normal way, then drew in a breath, bent lower and whispered, 'She only touched the hem of his garment.' That was *amazing*! He'd hit the bull's eye twice. And God answered his prayer on both counts.

Getting started

A major area of Satan's attack is to make you believe that you cannot hear God. Why? Because the devil is always afraid of those who live in vital contact with God. It is only when you live in constant communication with the living God that your life and ministry can advance with authority and confidence. That is the reason why in both war and peace, radio and telecommunications are so vital. When a coup takes place in some Third

World nation, the first thing that is captured is the radio station. If you have possession of the communications network you are in control.

How can you have the assurance that God will speak to you and that you will hear Him?

- First, because He has told you through His word: 'He who belongs to God hears what God says.' [John 8:47]
- Secondly, on examination of the experience of your own life you will discover that you have already heard God many times and in many ways. However, if at this present time you are not hearing God, it may be that discouragement or disobedience have blocked your spiritual ears.
- Thirdly, because this chapter may reveal to you certain ways God has already been using to try to get through to you.

The Pillar and the Ground of Truth

The foundation and touchstone of all our listening to God will be the Bible. God speaks to us through His word and we need to live in it daily, if we are to remain in the centre of His will. It is important to develop a habit of consistent and regular reading of Scripture. It is my normal practice to read the Bible through once each year. Such is my belief in the vital necessity of consistent Bible reading, that I have written and published a Bible Reading Plan entitled *If you want to Grow* which will take you through the Bible in One or Two Years. Each day you read a Psalm or part of Proverbs, a chapter of the New Testament and two chapters from the old Testament.[12]

All that we hear in other ways needs to be tested by, and to be in harmony with, the Scriptures. The Bible is the revelation of the triune God to His own people. It is not merely a doctrinal statement concerning the Christian life or a history of God's people.

The Pharisees had the same Scriptures as Jesus did; yet they made those scriptures a code that bound them and their followers so that Jesus said to them: 'You diligently study the Scriptures because you think that by them you possess eternal life. These are the Scriptures that testify about me, yet you refuse to come to me to have life.' [John 5:39-40]

Contrast that with the scene on the Emmaus road when we see Jesus handling the same Scriptures. 'And beginning with Moses and all the Prophets, he explained to them what was said in all the Scriptures concerning himself' [Luke 24:27]. And notice the response of those two

12   *If you want to grow*, A daily plan for reading
      through the Bible in either one or two years,
      Charles Sibthorpe, 222 Publications 1995

disciples: 'Were not our hearts burning within us while he talked with us on the road and opened the Scriptures to us? [v. 32].

You will see that it is possible to read the Bible without necessarily hearing God. We can hear Him through the Scriptures, but it needs faith and expectancy. Faith believes that God wants to speak each day through the Bible. Expectancy believes that He will speak today, because God is always true to His word.

In the front of the Bible Plan I have outlined three ways you can read the Bible.

1. *Take a shower* 'As the rain and the snow come down from heaven, and do not return to it without watering the earth and making it bud and flourish, so that it yields seed for the sower and bread for the eater, so is my word.' [Isaiah 55:10-11].
    Simply read the Bible passages set out for the day, asking God to speak, encourage and strengthen you. Do not worry about the things you do not understand. God's word will refresh and cleanse you as you take your daily shower in the Word.

2. *Be a student* 'Study to show yourself approved unto God, a workman ...

rightly handling the word of truth.'
[2 Timothy 2:15]
Seek to spend a little more time on part
of your daily reading so that you can
concentrate on each verse. Marking the
scriptures with various coloured pencils
is a great way of helping to draw
attention to what is being said and how
it affects you personally. (I use a
colouring method myself as I find it aids
concentration.)

3.   *Let it go deeper* 'Blessed is the man . .
. (whose) delight is in the law of the
Lord, and on his law he meditates day
and night.' [Psalm 1:1-2]
As you read your Bible always look for
a verse or phrase that you can take hold
of for that particular day and use it as a
basis for meditation. Write it down in a
notebook and encourage yourself by
what it says. You will find that it helps
to develop faith and gives you added
sharpness in your life.

It is important to read the Bible for your own
encouragement and strengthening, not merely as
preparation for sermons. The word opens
avenues, through which God can speak to you.

The psalmist says: 'Your word is a lamp to my feet and a light for my path' [Psalm 119:105].

'Blessed is the man who listens to me'

Taking time each day to sit quietly in the presence of God, to listen and write down what I hear has now become a regular part of my personal daily time with God. But it was not always so.

I remember that my first reaction was very negative. For a start, writing down things that God was speaking to me seemed to suggest that the Bible was incomplete. I also could not believe that God was sufficiently interested to speak to me; perhaps others, but not me.

This practice began during my time working with Colin Urquhart and was a principle he taught and recommended to the whole fellowship. Having been instructed and encouraged, in obedience I decided to have a go.

Feeling not a little foolish, I opened my notebook and prayed: 'Father, will you speak to me concerning my life today and about your will for me?' I picked up my pen and began to write. I did not hear an audible voice, but just had a sense that certain things were being impressed upon me. I wrote them down. I wrote about six lines in my book. Looking over what I had written, I felt a little foolish. Had I made it up? Had God really spoken to me? I closed the book and began to read the Scriptures and to pray concerning the day ahead, thinking no more about what I had written.

The next morning I felt somewhat discouraged at the thought of continuing this exercise and reluctantly opened up the notebook. As I read over the previous day's writing I was amazed. What I had written down was totally relevant to what had happened the day before. God had spoken! A sense of joy and relief flowed over me and I eagerly reached out for my pen and quietly waited for God to speak again.

As I have become more familiar with hearing God's voice in this way, I have realised that what I write down is similar to prophecy, which the Scriptures teach is not an addition to the Bible but given, as Paul writes 'for strengthening, encouragement and comfort' [1 Corinthians 14:3]. Like prophecy, anything heard and written down is not perfect but needs to be tested by the body of Christ: 'For we know in part and we prophesy in part' [1 Corinthians 13:9].

Listening to God daily has now become a most productive and creative part of my life. I believe it is vital for all who are called to leadership and ministry to cultivate this regular habit of waiting quietly in God's presence and listening to His voice. 'Blessed is the man who listens to me, watching daily at my doors, waiting at my doorway.' [Proverbs 8:34]

For a fuller and more detailed explanation about practically listening to God, you need to read the book written by my wife entitled *Can you hear God?*[13]

What do I hear as I listen each day? When I sit quietly before God, the first thing he shows me is anything needing correction. This will lead me to repentance. When I am out of sorts with God or my family I find it very difficult to tune in, as I know I will hear nothing until I have put things right both with Him and others.

Waiting quietly in the presence of God is not a passive exercise. In every conversation there will always be a two-way flow. If I want answers from God, I need to ask Him questions. So I will present the various situations in my life to God and ask what I need to know about them. On some issues I hear an immediate answer which I write down. Other questions may remain unanswered. I know that His answer will come when the time is right. What I do is to keep asking the same question and I discover as the days go by that God does unfold His answer and His direction as I continue in faithful obedience to Him. If I am not getting through I may well be asking the wrong questions.

13   *Can you hear God?*, Joyce Sibthorpe,
New Wine Press 1995

I seldom read back more than one or two days and I dispense with my notebook when it is full. To constantly be looking back places more emphasis on past words than on the freshness of God's voice for today. If I find it difficult to hear anything, I do glance back a day or two to discover if there are things God has said that I have failed to obey. I find God will not waste words on the disobedient. I know that what I write is not perfect, therefore do not put too much weight on one day's listening, but find that the things God repeatedly says to me are most important.

When the issues involve the Church, I expect that what I am hearing will be in harmony with what God is saying to my fellow-leaders. God speaks with a common voice and it is important that there is unity and harmony, particularly when major decisions are to be made.

Time spent quietly in the presence of God is essential for developing a listening ear. As pressures grow it is good to get away into a quiet place and allow God to minister peace into your heart and to speak into the situation. Time given to him is never wasted. 'He wakens me morning by morning, wakens my ear to listen like one being taught' [Isaiah 50:4].

Listening in Action

What has been said up to this point is like the training process; it is the aerobics class, it is time in the gym pumping iron, it is hitting balls on the golf driving-range. It will have limited value unless it is put to practice in the real game.

One morning, just as we were about to begin our daily prayer time in the Fellowship, I had a very strong impression that I should pray and ask for God's protection over us all. I asked everyone to stand, and as I started I found that the Holy Spirit was urging me in strong authoritative prayer. I began to bind powers of darkness, and to pronounce protection over all the families and the children. I continued praying for a lot longer than I had anticipated. I had begun so promptly that it had surprised a number of the Fellowship who were standing outside the door waiting for me to finish.

Unknown to me a drama was unfolding outside the door. As one of the leaders of the Fellowship waited, he noticed some liquid leak out of a parcel being carried by a young lady, whom we had rescued from a cult. She had only returned that morning from a weekend away with friends. Noone knew it at the time, but she had in fact returned from the cult who had sent her back with a petrol bomb which she had been instructed to throw into the midst of the meeting. The liquid was petrol escaping from the device which was intended to burst into flames in the meeting. She was hastily taken off to the bathroom where the plot was uncovered, the bomb made safe and the meeting continued with most of us, including me, none the wiser.

Later I was asked why I had prayed in such a way at that time. I cannot fully explain it, except to say that it was the fruit of listening to His voice and being sensitive to the urging of the Holy Spirit.

Keep tuned in

As I write this, we at Living Waters Church in Clevedon, where I am the pastor, are seeking to acquire a building for our growing congregation. The Church was planted about five years ago and has grown from 30 to more than 200. We have used a school and rented offices up to the present. About eight months ago we started exploring the possibility of buying a redundant cinema to convert into a worship centre. We looked over the building, prayed, listened to God and made an offer. To our utter amazement there was a public outcry, 10,000 signature petitions were given to the council and 250 protest letters landed on my desk. Our offer was accepted, but every delaying tactic was put in our way. We battled on, refusing to let the devil win. This surely was a clash of the kingdoms. Five months passed and still the battle raged. We now had entered a new year and could see no signs of progress. As we listened to God He told us that we could proceed when the lights went green, and on two counts we were at a red light.

At this point it would have been easy to become stubborn and declare that come what may, we would win through. However, as I continued to listen to God, I began to perceive a note of caution rising in my spirit. God spoke to me from a number of sources; there was a newspaper report estimating the real costs of converting the cinema; there was a shortfall in finance; there was a chance remark from a pastor friend of mine on a completely different subject; there was a word of prophecy.

We were then directed to a warehouse that had been empty for six years and would potentially meet all our needs. Why had we not seen this before? Most of the Church were very excited with this new opportunity, but a few were adamant that we must have the cinema. I desperately needed to hear God.

What did God have to say? I didn't find a ready answer as I tried to sit quietly and listen, so I turned to the scriptures and my readings for the day. The Old Testament reading was from Job. I was not expecting any mighty revelation as I turned to the passage. It was Job chapter 36, and I began to read verse by verse, then as I turned the page in my Bible, verse 16 exploded upon me, 'He is wooing you from the jaws of distress to a spacious place free from restriction, to the comfort of your table laden with choice food.' Hallelujah! God had spoken.

We are still in the process of negotiations, so I am not able to tell you the end of the story. All I can say is that, concerning the whole project, I remain with my ears open to God.

God's word assures us that as we obediently and faithfully follow Him we will know peace, fruitfulness and direction. The psalmist says: 'Great peace have they who love your law, and nothing can make them stumble' [Psalm 119:165]. Peace is not the absence of conflict, but a gift of God in the midst of the hurly-burly of life. If having faithfully followed through the principles of listening to God and seeking him daily you are left with a great lack of peace, you may well ask: *What is God trying to say now?* It is important to check out this restlessness with others, because it can occur for a number of different reasons. A lack of peace is one way in which we hear God. It may be over some small thing that needs to be put right, but it may be on account of something important that has a bearing on the whole direction of the situation.

Of all men, leaders need to know where they are going. If they have no purpose or direction, neither will those who are led. When the blind lead the blind, it always ends in disaster. If you know your life to be aimless, then you need to come before God fearlessly to hear what He has to say and be prepared to obey Him. The true

voice of authority will come only from one who
has cultivated the skill and habit of listening.

Cultivate the habit of listening

1. Can you hear God? Make sure that you are able to say a resounding **'yes'** to that question. If not, you may urgently need to read Joyce's book[14].

2. Do you have a satisfactory and systematic method of reading the Bible? Find a strategy that you are comfortable with and stick to it. It may vary from time to time but don't lapse into simply reading your favourite passages.

3. Develop your sensitivity to God's voice in all the situations and circumstances that surround you.

4. Don't stop listening until you have finished the task. Always be prepared to hear something new. God's word is a living word.

14 *Can you hear God?*, Joyce Sibthorpe, New Wine Press 1995

SCRIPTURAL AUTHORITY

My message and my preaching were not with wise and persuasive words, but with a demonstration of the Spirit's power.
[1 Corinthians 2:4]

A WORD FROM THE HEART

I came to realize that the Gifts of the Spirit as described in 1 Corinthians 12 are simply God's tool bag to get the job done,

Chapter 10

Living in the dimension of the Spirit

For me it all began with a Bible that was held together with red sticky tape. The Bible belonged to my sister Carolyn who had just returned from college in Cheltenham with the news that she had been filled with the Holy Spirit. There was no doubt that something had happened to her - she had a new sense of joy and peace and shared with me her fresh love for God's word. She also said that she now prayed in tongues, which did not impress me one bit.

My theology had been challenged. I was taught that I had received everything at conversion, and so my response to Carolyn was warm but defensive.

'I am glad that you have had this new experience of God,' I said, 'but I don't believe I need such an experience in order to draw closer to God or to know more of His power.' Carolyn's reaction was gracious and loving; she did not try to change my mind, but her new enthusiasm for Jesus kept tumbling out.

The youth fellowship, which was held in part of our home, was going really well. Over the previous five years we had seen it grow from twenty-five to well in excess of 150. Young people were becoming Christians almost every week, in fact you might say I was in the middle of a real success-story, but something nagged away inside me and I knew that there was a real lack in my Christian life.

Every time Carolyn returned home from college, there was that tattered Bible stuck together with more and more red sticky tape. And yet my own Bible was suffering from neglect rather than over-use.

Carolyn and Joyce were getting their heads together, and Joyce seemed quite enthusiastic to know this new power of the Holy Spirit for herself. I dug in my heels and determined that I would get through in my own way.

Meanwhile, I kept meeting people in whom I recognized a really close walk with God. When I began to talk to them in greater detail, I found that each one could point back to a time when they had been filled, or baptized in, the Holy Spirit.

The success of the youth fellowship continued, but I knew in my heart that I had taken the youngsters as far as I could. I remember one night kneeling down beside my bed feeling deeply discouraged by the emptiness of my own walk with God. 'Lord,' I said, 'unless you do something new in me, I have nothing more to give these kids.'

God seemed to be closing in on me. Joyce and I had become friendly with the new curate of Camborne, Barry Kissell, and his wife Mary. Here again were people who had that special something about them. I did not bother to ask what it was – I knew what the answer would be!

Barry and some of his friends had organised a young people's holiday in Northern Ireland and had persuaded Joyce, myself and a few of our young people to join them.

Carolyn managed to get in on the act too, and so it was that we set off in my car with six-month-old Daniel in a carry-cot in the back. Friends had kindly agreed to care for our two older children, Craig and Joanna.

Throughout the journey Carolyn and Joyce were in deep discussion about this infilling of the Holy Spirit. How does it happen? What is the effect? By this time, I was thoroughly bored by the whole subject. Nearly two years had elapsed since Carolyn had challenged me. The cry of my heart now was: 'Lord, please let it happen, or let it go away and never be spoken of again.'

The first few days of the holiday reassured me. No one tried to buttonhole me and lay hands on me, and for a while I thought it all might subside and be forgotten. And yet my feelings were not of relief but of potential disappointment, for I knew the emptiness and powerlessness of my relationship with God.

Things began to happen one day as we were sitting together in the quiet room of the conference centre. Joyce innocently turned to Barry and said: 'Would you tell us how you were filled with the Holy Spirit?' And so, in an entirely unemotional way, Barry unfolded his story. As he finished, Joyce calmly spoke out again: 'Would you pray with **us** to be filled with the Holy Spirit?' She had not asked me if I wanted to be included in the **us!**

Barry could see the surprise written all over my face, so he turned towards me and said: 'Charles, do you want me to pray with you?' My surprise quickly changed to relief as I replied: 'Yes I would like you to.'

Barry explained that to receive the infilling of the Holy Spirit was as simple as receiving Christ as Saviour. You simply had to ask, to receive by faith and to thank God for fulfilling his promise.

Joyce was prayed for first and Barry asked me to join with him in laying on hands. Nothing spectacular occurred, there was simply a tremendous sense of peace and the presence of Jesus. Joyce then joined Barry to lay hands on me and to pray. At that moment I felt nothing, I simply received by faith and gladly spoke out my thanks to God. I was relieved there had been no fireworks, and glad it had happened. But what in fact had happened?

By the time we reached our bedroom we both knew that something important had taken place. There was a deep sense of the presence of God and joy I had not known before. There had been times after a stirring meeting when I had felt inspired and resolved to follow God more closely, but by the morning my feelings had gone and my resolve had evaporated. How would I now feel in the morning?

When I woke I knew that God's Holy Spirit had done something in me that could not be removed by sleep or time, I had walked through a doorway into a deeper understanding of God.

A new dimension

I had now stepped into a new dimension of my walk with God. I had entered the realm of the Spirit, where I was soon to understand that unless God's power was working through me nothing of value could be achieved. Paul has brilliantly expressed what it means to minister in the power of the Spirit:

> My message and my preaching were not with wise and persuasive words, but with a demonstration of the Spirit's power, so that your faith might not rest on men's wisdom but on God's power. [1 Corinthians 2:4f]

That crisis-experience was for me a baptism into the power of God. It is sadly possible however, in these days when the work of the Holy Spirit is widely accepted, for leaders to embrace these things without having a distinct, powerful and personal encounter with the Holy Spirit. To be 'baptized in water', means you get WET and testify to the salvation you have received in Christ. To be 'baptized in Holy Spirit' should mean you get POWER.

Recently, I was convicted that it was possible for members of my own Church to have missed out on this dynamic experience, so once again I preached on being baptized in Holy Spirit and to my surprise more than 20 responded for prayer.

It is possible for people within our Churches to enjoy the presence of the Holy Spirit, and to enter into spontaneous worship without having received a personal and powerful encounter with the Holy Spirit. Here are the steps you need to take to receive this baptism of power:

1. *Know the truth of God's word:* Turn to the scriptures that speak of God's desire for every one of His children to be filled with the Holy Spirit. A. W. Tozer said:

    Before you are filled with the Holy Spirit you must be sure that you can be filled. The church has tragically neglected this great liberating truth – that there is now for the child of God a full and wonderful and completely satisfying anointing with the Holy Ghost. The Spirit-filled life is not a special, de-luxe edition of Christianity. It is part and parcel of the total plan of God for his people.[15]

2. *Repentance:* If you have been relying upon human strength and intellect, rather than God's power, this will need to be brought to God in repentance.

3. *Ask:* Jesus said, 'Everyone who asks receives.' You need to be specific. Vague prayers receive vague answers.

4. *Thanksgiving and Praise:* Thank God that your prayer has been answered and expect to receive spiritual gifts, especially speaking in tongues.

Speaking in Tongues

I have to admit that I was somewhat relieved that when Barry prayed for me I did not immediately

15   *How to be filled with the Holy Spirit*, **The Best of A W Tozer**, Kingsway 1983

speak in tongues; however, not many days had passed before I had a deep desire to receive this gift. Having been baptized into God's power I did not want to miss out on anything that He had for me. I again asked for some time with Barry, and as we prayed together God released His prayer language within me. I believe that everyone who is baptized in the Holy Spirit can speak in tongues; sadly, not all do.

Not many days had passed before I was to value this new gift. It happened while I was at work in the family business. Suddenly my father burst through the door of my office with the news that a young boy in our Church, a son of one of the key families, had been rushed into hospital with a burst appendix. His life was in danger and we had been asked to pray. As I sat there stunned by this piece of news, I could find no words to pray for this crisis. It was then that I realised that my prayer language was bubbling up inside of me ready to communicate with heaven. God had given the burden for intercession and He was now giving the words that would express what my own language could not.

> We do not know what we ought to pray for, but the Spirit himself intercedes for us with groans that words cannot express ... because the Spirit intercedes for the saints in accordance with God's will. [Romans 8:26f]

The boy received surgery, was admitted to the intensive care ward, the situation remained critical, and the prayers of the Church continued. As each day passed, the situation improved and sooner than anyone had expected he was back to normal.

In 1 Corinthians 14:4 Paul states that: 'He who speaks in a tongue edifies himself.' With all the stresses and strains of our modern world I have found this to be an immense value. One time when I was ministering in Austria and staying at the home of a doctor, he described to me the incredible demands of his work and the difficulty he found at the end of a very stressful day. I asked whether he ever used his prayer language to help the situation, to which he replied, 'No.' So I suggested that he obtain a good supply of worship cassettes to use in his car, and that on returning home from work he listen to a worship cassette and pray in tongues all the way home. The following evening he walked into the house with a beaming smile on his face bearing testimony that this had succeeded.

We lay such emphasis on training, education and the acquiring of skills that we are in danger of placing more credibility on expertise, than upon the power of God. The authority that we have for life and ministry is totally dependent upon God.

Many of you will have read the story of the ministry of Jackie Pullinger in Hong Kong. She very quickly realized that she was totally ineffective without the dynamic power of the Holy Spirit. Speaking in tongues became her moment by moment tool, to keep her in the protection of God, to lead her to the right people and then to see them released from their life-threatening addictions.

The Tools of the Trade

Once I began moving in the dimension of the Holy Spirit, I began to hear prophecies, tongues and interpretation in meetings; words of knowledge were being spoken out to release faith for healing (as demonstrated in the ministry of Eddie Smith) and discernment concerning powers of darkness that were in operation in people, which recognition would open the way for the ministry of deliverance. To begin with, these seemed mysterious and unattainable but I was soon to realise that this was far from the truth – a deception, in fact, that the devil would love to communicate to all God's people. As my understanding and experience increased, I came to realize that the Gifts of the Spirit as described in 1 Corinthians 12 are simply God's tool bag to get the job done, and are available for every Spirit filled believer. So, in faith, I began to reach out to God for these gifts that could release more of God's authority in my life and ministry.

I was taking a ministers' and leaders' conference in Sweden, where we had seen God at work dealing deeply with all those present. At the time healing was not a significant part of my ministry, but on the last evening I had a strong impression that God wanted to heal physical conditions among the people in the conference. The more I prayed the stronger the impression became, so I spoke out, 'I believe that God wants to heal people physically here tonight.' I then found myself saying, 'Now God is going to show me what he wants to heal, and as I speak it out you need to respond and be prayed for.'

At that moment I had received nothing, but had confidently spoken in faith trusting in the faithfulness of God. A few moments passed with nothing happening – it seemed like an eternity; I then began to feel a pain at the base of my neck. *What's happening to me*, I thought, and suddenly it dawned upon me that God was speaking to me in the same way as He had spoken to Eddie Smith, He was giving me a physical sensation to indicate a healing condition. So I spoke it out and waited, looking around the room; for I moment it seemed there would be no response when a pastor's wife spoke out, 'It's my neck that needs healing.' *Hallelujah!* I breathed a sigh of relief and went over and prayed with her. Other sensations followed and I spoke them out; there were about 4 or 5, and I prayed for each one. Everyone was rejoicing as the conference reached its climax and all returned home testifying to God's power.

I was thrilled to have seen a breakthrough in authority in this area of healing, but I desperately needed to know that the healing had been genuine. Some months later, we had a group of Swedish pastors visiting one of our Leaders' Weeks in England. One the first evening as they gathered, I was greeted by the pastor's wife mentioned earlier. Her face wreathed in smiles, she stood in front of me and gave testimony to the healing that had been released in her neck. My faith was greatly strengthened and I was given boldness to take bigger risks in future. I heard this statement recently concerning the use of the Gifts, 'If you've got the bottle, He's got the power.'

Not resting on men's wisdom - but on God's power

When you have been in ministry for a number of years, many will seek you out for wisdom and counsel. This happens particularly when you are abroad. It is all too possible to reach back into the past and give advice based upon years of experience rather than seek a word from God, which will release His wisdom into the situation.

One particular situation that comes to mind happened in Hungary. Joyce and I had been taking a Pastor's Retreat in a house on the shores of Lake Balaton; it had been an intense time and we were physically and mentally exhausted. We had now returned to the home of our hosts in Budapest and were lying down for a rest, looking forward to a relaxed evening meal with our hosts, when there was a knock at our door. A pastor from the east of the country had travelled many miles to come and see me and was waiting in the living-room of our hosts. I groaned inwardly. All my resources were spent, but out of a heart of compassion I went to pray with him.

The pastor was in great distress; he believed that he had failed God through disobedience, and that a recent theft from his home was God's judgement on him because of his failure. I first needed to minister forgiveness to him and assure him that God does not take revenge upon our mistakes, but forgives and restores. The tears flowed as forgiveness was received. The sticking point was that he could see no future and he felt he had cut himself off from the voice of God. All my pleading with him was unsuccessful and this dear man sat in front of me – a picture of misery. *I can't send a man away like this,* I desperately cried out to God. Almost immediately a word came into my mind, 'Jonah'; I was about to dismiss it as being irrelevant when it came again. Slowly the light dawned. Jonah was in a parallel situation, he had failed and thought God was finished with him. But in Jonah 3:1 it says: 'And the word of the Lord came again to Jonah *a second time.'* I reached for my Bible and showed the verse to him. Light dawned, the load lifted, his face changed. I could clearly see that he had been transformed from despair to hope, from sadness to joy. We prayed the word of the Lord into his heart and he left a changed man.

> The word of God is living and active. Sharper than any double-edged sword, it penetrates even to dividing soul and spirit, joints and marrow; it judges the thoughts and attitudes of the heart. [Hebrews 4:12]

Worship, Word and Wonders

When God led us to plant Living Waters Church He impressed upon us three foundational principles.

1. First, we should give unhurried time to praise and worship, knowing from Scripture that God is 'enthroned on the praises of His people' [Psalm 22:3]. We have been greatly blessed from the beginning with many very anointed musicians. Within the worship time we seek to leave space where the spoken Gifts of the Spirit can operate.

2. The second principle is the anointed preaching of the Word, because 'faith comes by hearing and hearing by the word of God' [Romans 10:17]. This is

always central, because no matter what amazing things may be happening, unless we continue to hold the word as our yardstick, we will become vulnerable to excess and error.

3.   The third principle is Wonders. We always leave time and are available to pray with people within the context of the service. We have seen remarkable healings and life transformation. In fact very little counselling takes place in our Church because most needs are met in the ministry time in our normal services.

Not with wise and persuasive words…but with a demonstration of the Spirit's power. [1 Corinthians 2:4]

The Anointing

The true mark of authority on the life of a leader is the anointing of God. I can *appoint* any person I like to preach or function in an area of leadership, but it is only God who can pour out His *anointing* as a confirmation that the right person has been chosen and that he is operating in the ministry God has ordained for him.

Anointing in Scripture has its roots in the old Covenant where the priests and kings were anointed with oil as they took up office.

The mark of God's anointing is similarly upon lives and ministries today. It has three characteristics: first it indicates the *confirmation of God* upon a life and role in ministry. An anointed life is one that is totally submitted to the authority of God, and anointed ministry flows out of that relationship with God and the specific call He gives.

You need to operate within the call that has come from God. For example, if God has called you to be an evangelist and you try to become a teacher, you will not enjoy God's anointing on your teaching, for God will not anoint something He has not initiated.

This does not mean that roles and ministries cannot change; they do, but only under God's direction.

Secondly, anointing is a mark of the *authority of God*. As you fulfil your calling and divine appointment you need to seek God's specific anointing upon each aspect of the work. When the anointing comes upon you, you will be conscious of a level of authority that can only come from God. Both you and others will know that such authority does not stem from human capability.

Thirdly, anointing reveals the *character of God*. As you are obedient to your call and live in total dependence upon Him, He will be glorified and his character will be revealed. Human sweat, fuss and striving will be absent and the sense of God's peace and blessing will be very evident. This is essential for all who preach and minister, but is equally necessary for more basic roles.

True anointing always bring glory to God, not to man.

Moving in the power of the Spirit

1. Have you been baptised in Holy Spirit? I
    have deliberately left out 'the' because it
    adds emphasis. The evidence will be
    God's power in your life and ministry.

2. Do you speak in tongues? If not, why not? It
    is an indispensable tool in the life of a
    leader. It is a key the opens the door to
    other gifts.

3. 'Eagerly desire spiritual gifts' is what Paul
    said to the Church at Corinth. Is it true
    of you, and what gifts are you using?

4. Take time to understand what is true
    anointing. If you want to have real
    spiritual authority, it is essential to know
    how to receive and operate under the
    anointing of God.

SCRIPTURAL AUTHORITY

Husbands be considerate as you live with your wives . . . so that nothing will hinder your prayers. [1 Peter 3:7]

A WORD FROM THE HEART

You cannot strengthen your ministry and leadership by your performance in the pulpit or your handling of the Church council, but by the things which no one except God sees.

Chapter 11

The Hidden Things

I had been invited to speak to a Conference of Baptist Pastors in Northern Germany. I had two colleagues with me: Jens had come to lead praise and worship (he was later to become my son-in-law); Steffan, also a German Baptist Pastor, was my interpreter. He is a close friend and fully committed to my ministry. I thought the conference delegates would have learned enough about me to know the kind of message I would bring.

We began our first session with a time of worship, led by Jens. He did brilliantly with a group who were totally unfamiliar with free worship and sat woodenly in front of us. I preached about the cross and the heart response of the leader towards God. At the end I attempted to lead in a time of prayer and seeking God.

'That was a tough evening,' I said to Jens as we arrived back in our bedroom, 'I wonder what they made of us?'

I was soon to find out, as we were summoned to meet the organizing committee immediately after breakfast. The opening was abrupt, 'We don't like the songs, we don't like the preaching, and we don't like your style of ministry. We would like you to give us your opinions; we will then give you our opinions to be followed by discussion.'

They expressed themselves very succinctly. I thought for a moment and then replied, 'I thought we had come here to meet with God. I am not really interested in your opinions, I am not particularly interested in my own opinions, but I do believe that we need to hear from God.'

'– However,' I added after there had been more tedious discussion, 'I do not want to be obstructive and after the next session I would be happy to open up a discussion.' Peace was restored and after some further conversation we dispersed.

Back in my room I cried out to God: 'What am I to preach about next?' For some time I struggled, feeling the immense pressure being placed on me. I thought about all sorts of interesting teaching, but could find no peace. At last God spoke into my heart, 'You need to speak about 'The hidden things'; the areas of life that no-one sees and yet are the foundation for authority in ministry.'

As I continued to listen to God, I found myself directed to three key topics. That evening as I stood up to speak, I began with the vital need for a sanctuary where we daily meet with God; I continued with family, where my holiness is on show 24 hours a day; and I concluded with the necessity of walking in the light, including my own personal testimony of gaining victory over sexual temptation and also my willingness to humble myself before others. I had shared my heart and the word went deeply into their hearts. Darkness and need was exposed, and when I concluded and attempted to open up a discussion, there was silence. After some minutes they began to bang their tables, not in protest as it would be in England, but a German custom which is equivalent to warm and heartfelt applause. There was no discussion, God had spoken and the only valid response was towards Him.

You cannot strengthen your ministry and leadership by your performance in the pulpit or your handling of the Church council, but by the things which no one sees.

Do you remember those old car batteries which had a row of screw caps on top giving access to the individual cells? They needed to be replenished with distilled water at regular intervals, and if neglected the acid would evaporate and the battery fail. When that happened, an examination of the cells normally revealed that everything was in perfect order, except for one cell, which would be dry with horribly twisted plates. Only one cell had failed, and yet the whole battery had lost its power. It is not the outward things that are most likely to undermine your leadership and ministry, but unseen areas of life.

Sanctuary

I am using the word 'Sanctuary' to describe the place where daily I meet with God. It is not sermon preparation time, it is not administration; it is time spent with God, in worship, listening to him, feeding upon his word and prayer. This is the place of power, this is where my authority is developed.

When our eldest son Craig was about 19, he went to the States for a Discipleship School with Youth with a Mission. This was to be a life changing time and took place on a base in the foothills of the Rocky Mountains. During the last month of his year abroad, we and our other children joined him for a holiday visiting family and friends. As we were being shown around the base, Craig took us into the boiler house to point out a corner where he went each day for his time with God. Winters in Colorado are extremely cold, and a place of peace and solitude, which is also warm, was not easy to find. He told us that it required early rising to ensure that one of his fellow students had not pinched his spot.

Something very important, which remains a daily habit, was being established in the heart of my son Craig; 'Sanctuary'. You may call it by a different name, but the principle remains; unless there is a place where we meet with God day by day, we will lack the true foundations to a life that is fruitful and powerful.

A few years back, I recall talking with a friend and leader at the time everyone was flocking to 'Power Evangelism' and 'Power Healing' conferences. He said, 'The conferences are great, but I fear that too many people are hoping for a short cut to power. They desire *power without intimacy.*'

Family

The first place where all my beliefs and life principles are tested is among my family. My wife is the first person with whom I walk in the light. Confessing my faults to the one who knows me best of all, liberates me to be open before others, including my children, household and the rest of the body of Christ.

Because my marriage is the primary place of openness in my life, it is where the principles of love, acceptance and forgiveness are established. My faithfulness towards God will be proved by my fidelity in marriage, a vital principle for all who are called to lead others. 'Husbands love your wives, just as Christ loved the Church' [Ephesians 5:25], is not simply theology, it is a command of God.

Joyce is the one with whom I share the strongest bond of unity, stronger even than with my fellow church leaders. That makes our relationship a powerful place of prayer. Jesus said: 'I tell you that if two of you on earth agree about anything you ask for, it will be done for you by my father in heaven' [Matthew 18:19]. Agreeing in prayer is not merely a formula of words, but is a powerful dynamic that flows out of hearts that are in complete unity.

In Peter's first letter he is exhorting men to be considerate as they live with their wives, not only because a man should be loving and caring, but also because a lack of consideration will hinder prayer [1 Peter 3:7].

I thank God for a warm, loving and mutually satisfying physical relationship in my marriage, based on giving and not on getting. This brings joy and strength to us both and denies the enemy a channel of temptation. It is tragic that many people called to Christian leadership have made shipwreck of their lives through moral sin. Often the reason is not simply insufficient resistance to the temptation, but lack of time given to building a strong and satisfying sexual relationship within their marriage. It has often been said: 'If there is peace in the bedroom there will be peace in the home.'

May I reiterate what we learned in Chapter 3 *A heart after God*? The first need of a Christian wife is to have a man whose heart is after God. That means you need to love God more than you love your wife. The more you love Him, the more His perfect love will pour through you to your wife, to your family and to others He has given you to love.

It is very important for the wife of a leader to know the call of God on her life as well as her husband's. That call will not be at variance with his, thereby creating conflict, but will have come to her direct from God.

Let me illustrate. Since God first called me into full-time ministry, there have been a number of changes of direction from God; for two years we worked in Cornwall, before moving to Sussex for eight years, to be followed by four years involved entirely in travelling, and then Church planting in Somerset. Each time it was very important for me to know that Joyce and I were in complete unity, knowing that God had spoken to us both, and were therefore both eager and ready to go. We were then able to share this with our children for whom the moves caused dislocation, as schools had to be changed and friends left behind. The unity God gave us paved the way for family unity, enabling us to move willingly together.

I have seen men lose a God-given ministry when their wives have undermined their vision, obedience or determination. It is not practical in Christian ministry for a couple to work on the 'you go your way and I'll go mine' principle. The result of that kind of situation will inevitably be weakness and failure. Let it also be said that I have seen women whose commitment to God's call on their lives has been stunted by their husbands!

The challenge of family life means that not only is the leader seeking to extend the kingdom of God out there, but is also seeking to see his children embrace the same truths in their lives. I have already stated how Joyce and I are deeply grateful to God that all our five children came to the point of personal commitment of their lives to God – and this despite, for most of our married life, having had folk, apart from our children, living within the family.

I well remember sharing this aspect of my life with those hard-bitten Baptist pastors in Northern Germany. I said something like this, 'It is quite a challenge to your holiness to be living 24 hours a day, not only in front of your family, but also before total strangers.' Those words seemed to hit the pastors like a sledge-hammer. The quality of the whole of life is vital; we should never be off duty when it comes to holiness.

The Wall

There are some bad character traits of which you are painfully aware and yet feel powerless to cure. For me, it all came to the surface when I was having a conversation with Colin Urquhart about pressure. We were trying to find an answer to the dilemma which seemed continuously to find me complaining about the demands both of work and family life. I seemed to be spending an immense amount of energy trying to fight my way into a space free from pressure.

'There must be a key somewhere to all this,' Colin mused, as our conversation continued. It then slowly began to dawn upon me that the root cause of the pressure was self-protection. I was trying to free myself from this pressure by pushing people away from me. The root of the problem was my selfishness which was not allowing people to get near to me. I saw a picture of myself with a high wall of protection built around me; Joyce was on the inside, but everyone else was outside. When anyone climbed the wall I felt pressurized and would satisfy their clamour simply to push them away from me. I was shocked and alarmed by what was slowly unfolding. Colin suggested that I go away and find some time to think and pray. I left the room gutted and deeply ashamed. I did not know how I could ever be of any use to God or man. I felt like asking Colin whether he could give me a job growing vegetables. The rest of the day was spent in complete turmoil.

I awoke very early the next morning battling with my thoughts. Was there any way through for me? As I lay half awake, half asleep, I became aware of a series of thoughts passing through my head, like a video replay of every area of selfishness in my entire life. I could see it now, and as each incident passed I cried out to God for forgiveness. When at last the picture faded from the screen, another emerged into my consciousness. I saw myself standing in the middle of a pile of building rubble, and as I looked more closely, I could see that the wall had been broken down. I felt free, yet incredibly vulnerable.

Just then Coralie, our younger daughter who must have been about eight or nine at the time, crept into our bedroom; it was Saturday morning when we attempted to have a bit of a lie-in. She would normally have climbed in on Joyce's side of the bed and gone to sleep. This day she came to my side, crawled in and snuggled up to me. 'That's incredible!' I thought, 'at the precise moment that God has finished doing a deep work in my heart, Coralie has come as a confirmation to show that she could detect a new availability, a new love and a new openness in me.'

It was a hidden work, yet very powerful, which released me to a new level of openness and proved to be a key to the ministry that would lie ahead. God can change your character.

The genuineness of this work of God in my life was confirmed by Rosie, one of the folk who lived in our family. She had lived with us during the first year of our time in the community. She then moved to another household, only to return to us two and a half years later. Rosie was with me on one occasion when I testified to what God had done in my life when He broke down the wall. On the way home she said, 'I can really confirm the truth of what you were saying this morning because you were so different when I returned to your household.' That statement greatly encouraged me because the test of true change will be in the way it is recognized by others.

The most profound changes in our lives happen hidden from public gaze, which I suppose, is what Paul was describing when he wrote, 'And we, who with unveiled faces all reflect the Lord's glory, are being transformed into his likeness with ever increasing glory, which comes from the Lord, who is the Spirit.' [2 Corinthians 3:18]

You will seek me and find me

1. Where is your 'Sanctuary?' Are you setting aside quality time to meet with God on a daily basis?

2. Are you living your message in your home and family? Are you giving adequate time to your spouse? Are you protecting areas of danger and vulnerability?

3. Do you want God to change your character? Are you prepared to be honest about your areas of weakness? Do you want to be different?

4. Are you willing to give God the time and availability to be changed by Him from one degree of glory to another?

Chapter 12

I thought you were the Boss

Authority is given by God to those called to leadership; however, unless we exercise the authority we have been given, we will remain ineffective.

Let me illustrate what I mean with this personal story. It happened to Trevor Hughes, a friend of mine, who is also a fellow-leader in Living Waters Church.

When Trevor left the British Army and returned home to Cardiff after completing his National Service in the early 1950s, he applied for work on the railway and was assigned to a gang whose task was to maintain the railtrack.

Being young and ambitious, when the opportunity came to gain promotion, he eagerly volunteered to become Sub-ganger, which made him second-in-command over a group of 24 men. His early enthusiasm quickly evaporated as these men, all of whom were older than Trevor, continuously ridiculed him and bucked his authority. After about six months he had had enough. He was in the process of coming to the decision to resign and revert to his former job, when on the evening before he had resolved to end this impossible predicament, he was sitting at home beside the fire with his wife June, reflecting upon the situation.

June had been largely unaware of the agony of the past weeks, and was quite surprised at what she was hearing. Looking up from the book she had been reading, she simply remarked, 'I thought you were the boss!' This innocently spoken remark exploded inside of him, and effected an amazing change.

Trevor now sat in his chair in stunned silence, thinking about the words June had just spoken. He had taken on a job which carried an authority that he had failed to exercise. This had caused great distress within him, but also was creating a gang of men who were constantly bickering and arguing, because everyone was doing their own thing. At that moment Trevor came to a fresh decision. He was not going to resign!

The next morning as he rode his bicycle towards Cardiff Railway Station, Trevor had become a different man. A quizzical smile broke upon his face as he travelled along the road thinking, 'There are 24 men riding their bicycles in the same direction as me and pondering how they are going to create another day of hassle and aggravation for Trev. Little do they know, everything is about to change!'

Cardiff Station was a buzz of activity because a Royal visit was imminent; Prince Philip, the Duke of Edinburgh was to visit a factory nearby and would be arriving at Cardiff in a few days time. Everything had to be perfect for his coming; the painters were already in action, and now the track-side needed to be spick and span. The chief ganger assigned Trevor and eight men to move four damaged concrete sleepers and bury them behind a shed.

Part of the aggravation caused by the men was an unwillingness to share any of their experience, and consequently assist in finding the best way of tackling a particular job. The usual pattern was to leave Trevor to devise his own course of action, and once the work was underway for the men to mutter among themselves a better way of accomplishing the task.

Nothing had changed in the minds of the men as they approached the four enormous lumps of concrete. Trevor had assessed the situation and directed the eight men to position themselves evenly around the sleeper and to carry it behind the shed, where a hole would be dug and the offending object would be buried out of sight. The usual mumbling commenced as they began to move the sleeper to its intended destination. It was heavier than anyone had anticipated and they struggled as they hauled their load. As they returned, breathing heavily, to tackle sleeper number two, their mumblings were more direct and pointed. 'Why don't we use the rollers, Trev?' The reply they received brought shock and amazement. 'No!' said Trevor, 'You will carry them all as you did the first one, and bury them as was decided at the commencement of this job. When you have finished, I need to talk to you.'

With much grumbling, grunting and groaning the task was completed, and immediately they gathered around Trevor listening intently. 'Ever since I took this job as Sub-Ganger,' he began, 'you have tried to make me look ridiculous and have failed to give me any advice. You all have a great deal more experience than I, and yet you have consistently withheld this expertise from me. From today everything has changed, once I have decided upon a course of action it will not be altered until the task is completed. If you know of a better way of doing any particular job, tell me before we start.'

The worm had turned! The boy had become the boss! The authority given by British Rail had been grasped and exercised. That gang which had gained a reputation for grumbling and discontent soon became the most efficient gang working out of Cardiff. What was formerly, 'every man doing that which was right in his own eyes' became a cohesive unit where everyone's energy and ideas were working to a common aim, under leadership. In fact, that day changed Trevor's life, he took the authority given to him, exercised it and eventually rose to become the Chief Training Officer in the West Region of British Rail.

As a Christian leader, you have been given authority by Jesus. If you fail to use this authority, you will not accomplish your God given assignment.

Hebrews 13:17 states,

> Obey your leaders and submit to their authority. They keep watch over you as men who must give an account. Obey them so that their work will be a joy, not a burden, for that would be of no advantage to you.

The call to leadership is a privilege; it is not for gain or prestige, but because of a God-given desire to see His kingdom come and His will be done. Many of the things in this book you may have found daunting and demanding – this is not meant as a deterrent: for although it may be tough, the exercise of authority and leadership for God is a joy.

* * * * * * *

Charles and Joyce Sibthorpe can be contacted c/o 222 Trust, Firbank. Wrington Road, Congresbury, Bristol BS21 5JG. On the next page, they are pleased to offer readers additional resources to help put into practice what you have read:

- *If You Want To Grow,* A daily plan for reading the whole Bible in one or two years (please send a cheque made out to '222 Publications' for £1).

- *Eagle Camp*, an annual summer camp based in South West England where families with children can seek spiritual and physical refreshing. Past guest speakers have included Reinhart Bonnke, Dr Bob Gordon and many others (Brochure available).

- *Monthly tape* of the teaching at Living Waters Church. Supplied free on a listen-and-return basis (a nominal charge is payable if you wish to keep any tape).

- *On Eagle's Wings*; Their ministry newsletter , which includes the details of Charles' leadership training work within the 222 Trust (the name is based on II Timothy 2:2 that focuses on building up leaders).

- *Weekly services* at Living Waters Church, in Clevedon 12 miles South of Bristol (please write for service details). Visitors welcome.